Corporate Finance in Asia and the COVID-19 Crisis

This work is published under the responsibility of the Secretary-General of the OECD. The opinions expressed and arguments employed herein do not necessarily reflect the official views of the Member countries of the OECD.

This document, as well as any data and map included herein, are without prejudice to the status of or sovereignty over any territory, to the delimitation of international frontiers and boundaries and to the name of any territory, city or area.

The statistical data for Israel are supplied by and under the responsibility of the relevant Israeli authorities. The use of such data by the OECD is without prejudice to the status of the Golan Heights, East Jerusalem and Israeli settlements in the West Bank under the terms of international law.

Note by Turkey
The information in this document with reference to "Cyprus" relates to the southern part of the Island. There is no single authority representing both Turkish and Greek Cypriot people on the Island. Turkey recognises the Turkish Republic of Northern Cyprus (TRNC). Until a lasting and equitable solution is found within the context of the United Nations, Turkey shall preserve its position concerning the "Cyprus issue".

Note by all the European Union Member States of the OECD and the European Union
The Republic of Cyprus is recognised by all members of the United Nations with the exception of Turkey. The information in this document relates to the area under the effective control of the Government of the Republic of Cyprus.

Please cite this publication as:
OECD (2022), *Corporate Finance in Asia and the COVID-19 Crisis*, OECD Publishing, Paris, https://doi.org/10.1787/87861cf0-en.

ISBN 978-92-64-36509-4 (print)
ISBN 978-92-64-69505-4 (pdf)
ISBN 978-92-64-83314-2 (HTML)

Photo credits: Cover © Andrew Esson/Baseline Arts Ltd.

Corrigenda to publications may be found on line at: www.oecd.org/about/publishing/corrigenda.htm.
© OECD 2022

The use of this work, whether digital or print, is governed by the Terms and Conditions to be found at https://www.oecd.org/termsandconditions.

Foreword

The COVID-19 crisis has led to unprecedented health, social and economic costs and has exacerbated vulnerabilities in economies around the world. Effective early steps by Asian economies to contain the pandemic cushioned the blow to the region's markets. Importantly, the fact that today over half of the world's listed companies are listed on an Asian stock exchange allowed them to tap into equity markets during the crisis on a large scale. During 2020 and 2021, more than 3 500 already-listed Asian companies were able to raise USD 669 billion from public equity markets.

Asian capital markets and corporations deserve special attention due to their importance in global markets, their integration into regional and global supply chains, and their ownership structures. With this in mind, this report analyses some of the long-term trends in Asia's listed corporate sector. It also looks at how Asian companies used market-based financing during the pandemic, and the main fiscal and regulatory measures Asian authorities took to support the corporate sector's access to finance during this period.

The report covers the main aspects of the capital market ecosystem in Asia:

- The first chapter provides an overview of the non-financial corporate sector over the last two decades. Using firm-level data, it offers analysis of corporate capital structures, performance and investment activity, as well as the use of market-based financing and the ownership structure of listed companies. It also shows long-term trends on how Asian companies have been using both equity and bond markets to raise capital.
- The second chapter shows how Asian companies were able to access financing by using equity and corporate bond markets during the COVID-19 pandemic. It also takes stock of the fiscal and regulatory measures implemented by Asian authorities to respond to the pandemic and mitigate the effects on the corporate sector.

Strengthening corporate sector resilience will require further efforts to adapt existing legal and regulatory frameworks so that capital markets can better play their role of channelling financial resources towards long-term investments. Corporate governance frameworks also need to be enhanced to provide investors, corporations and other stakeholders with tools and incentives adapted to the post COVID-19 environment.

The trends presented in this report and the initial impact on the corporate sector during the pandemic provide a starting point for understanding the long-term effects of the crisis and the challenges ahead for Asia's corporate sector.

 This report is part of the OECD Capital Market Series, which informs policy discussions on how capital markets can serve the important role of channelling financial resources from households into productive investments in the real economy.

A set of selected indicators and detailed description of data sources as well as the methodology for data collection are provided in the annex. This report has benefited from discussions with and feedback from participants in the OECD-Asia Roundtable on Corporate Governance.

The Review was prepared by a team led by Serdar Çelik, Acting Head of the Corporate Governance and Corporate Finance Division within the OECD Directorate for Financial and Enterprise Affairs, and composed of Thomas Dannequin, Adriana De La Cruz, Carl Magnus Magnusson, Alejandra Medina, Tugba Mulazimoglu and Yun Tang. The report benefited from the financial support of the Government of Japan.

Table of contents

Foreword 3

Acronyms and abbreviations 7

Executive summary 8

1 Corporate landscape 11
    1.1. Corporate sector overview: Capital structure, performance and investment 12
    1.2. Trends in the use of public equity 27
    1.3. Trends in the use of corporate bonds 33
    1.4. Trends in ASEAN capital markets 38
    1.5. Ownership structure of listed companies 40

2 Navigating the pandemic 47
    2.1. Market-based financing during the pandemic 48
    2.2. The impact of the COVID-19 crisis on corporate sales 60
    2.3. Government support programmes and regulatory measures in Asian economies 62

References 72

Annex A. Methodology for data collection and classification 74

Notes 79

FIGURES

Figure 1.1. Overview of non-financial listed companies in Asia 13
Figure 1.2. Operating efficiency and profitability of non-financial listed companies 14
Figure 1.3. Profitability of non-financial listed companies from selected Asian economies 15
Figure 1.4. Distribution of ROA of non-financial listed companies 15
Figure 1.5. Share of high-profitability non-financial listed companies by ROE 16
Figure 1.6. Leverage of non-financial listed companies 16
Figure 1.7. Distribution of leverage of non-financial listed companies 17
Figure 1.8. Debt-to-EBITDA ratio of non-financial listed companies 18
Figure 1.9. Debt level of non-financial listed companies by debt-to-EBITDA ratios 19
Figure 1.10. Debt ratio of non-financial listed companies by economy 20
Figure 1.11. Debt ratio of non-financial listed companies in Asia by industries 20
Figure 1.12. Zombie companies by economy / region 21
Figure 1.13. Corporate investment of non-financial listed companies by region 22
Figure 1.14. Corporate investment of non-financial listed companies in Asia 23
Figure 1.15. Corporate investment, average by industry (2011-20) 23
Figure 1.16. Dividends of non-financial listed companies 24
Figure 1.17. Bank lending versus debt securities in selected Asian economies 25

| 5

Figure 1.18. Capital structure of non-financial companies in selected economies as of end-2020 26
Figure 1.19. Non-performing loans ratio in selected regions 26
Figure 1.20. Non-performing loans ratio by jurisdiction 27
Figure 1.21. Initial public offerings, total amount raised 28
Figure 1.22. Top 20 jurisdictions by number of non-financial company IPOs between 2012 and 2021 29
Figure 1.23. Newly listed and delisted companies 30
Figure 1.24. Growth company IPOs' share in the total number of non-financial company IPOs 30
Figure 1.25. Non-domestic listed companies and host stock exchanges' jurisdiction as of end-2020 31
Figure 1.26. Distribution of IPO proceeds by industry (share in total proceeds, 2012-21) 31
Figure 1.27. Secondary public offerings, total amount raised 32
Figure 1.28. Distribution of SPO proceeds by industry (share in total proceeds, 2012-21) 33
Figure 1.29. Asian non-financial corporate bonds landscape 34
Figure 1.30. Credit quality of non-financial corporate bonds 35
Figure 1.31. Composition of investment grade issuance 35
Figure 1.32. Industry distribution of non-financial corporate bonds issued in Asia 36
Figure 1.33. Median issue size and distribution by size category 37
Figure 1.34. Distribution of corporate bond issuances by exchange and currency, 2000-21 38
Figure 1.35. Initial and secondary public offerings by ASEAN companies 39
Figure 1.36. Corporate bond issuances by ASEAN companies 39
Figure 1.37. Asia's share in global equity markets as of end-2020 40
Figure 1.38. Investors' holdings as of end-2020 41
Figure 1.39. Investors' holdings in Asian markets as of end-2020 41
Figure 1.40. Non-domestic ownership in Asian markets by category of investor as of end-2020 42
Figure 1.41. Ownership concentration by the largest three shareholders as of end-2020 43
Figure 1.42. Ownership concentration at the company level as of end-2020 43
Figure 2.1. Equity capital raised by non-financial companies in public markets in 2020 and 2021 49
Figure 2.2. IPOs by Asian non-financial companies in 2020 and 2021 by industry 50
Figure 2.3. Monthly initial public offerings by non-financial companies in 2020 and 2021 51
Figure 2.4. Initial public offerings by Asian non-financial companies in 2020 and 2021 52
Figure 2.5. IPOs by non-financial companies by industry 53
Figure 2.6 IPOs by non-financial companies by jurisdiction and industry 53
Figure 2.7. Monthly secondary public offerings by non-financial companies 54
Figure 2.8. Secondary public offerings by Asian non-financial companies 55
Figure 2.9. SPOs by non-financial companies by industry 56
Figure 2.10. SPOs by non-financial companies by jurisdiction and industry 57
Figure 2.11. Monthly corporate bond issuance by non-financial companies 58
Figure 2.12. Asian non-financial corporate bond issuance by jurisdiction 59
Figure 2.13. Asian non-financial corporate bond issuance by credit quality 59
Figure 2.14. Asian non-financial corporate bond issuance by industry 60
Figure 2.15. The COVID-19 crisis' impact on sales of listed corporations by economy/region 61
Figure 2.16. The COVID-19 crisis' impact on sales of listed companies by industry in Asia 62

TABLES

Table 1.1. Non-financial listed companies as of end-2020 12
Table 1.2. Corporations as owners by location and listed status as of end-2020 44
Table 1.3. Public sector holdings as of end-2020 45
Table 1.4. Listed companies in Asia under state control as of end-2020 46
Table 2.1. Indirect measures in response to COVID-19 64
Table 2.2. Direct measures in response to COVID-19 67
Table 2.3. Selected regulatory measures in response to COVID-19 70
Table 2.4. Insolvency and bankruptcy regulatory measures in response to COVID-19 71

Table A A.1. Economic sectors based on the Thomson Reuters Business Classification 75
Table A A.2. Categories of owners 77

Follow OECD Publications on:

 https://twitter.com/OECD

 https://www.facebook.com/theOECD

 https://www.linkedin.com/company/organisation-eco-cooperation-development-organisation-cooperation-developpement-eco/

 https://www.youtube.com/user/OECDiLibrary

OECD Alerts https://www.oecd.org/newsletters/

Acronyms and abbreviations

ADB	Asian Development Bank	IPO	initial public offering
AGM	annual general meeting	J-REITs	Japan real estate investment trusts
ASEAN	Association of Southeast Asian Nations	MAS	Monetary Authority of Singapore
BIS	Bank for International Settlements	NDRC	Chinese National Development and Reform Commission
BoJ	Bank of Japan	NPL	non-performing loan
BSEC	Bangladesh Securities and Exchange Commission	OECD	Organisation for Economic Co-operation and Development
BSF	Thailand Corporate Bond Stabilisation Fund	ONS	UK Office for National Statistics
Capex	capital expenditure	OTC	over-the-counter
CIT	corporate income tax	PENJANA	Malaysia Short-term National Economic Recovery Plan
CPI	consumer price index	R&D	research and development
CSRC	China Securities Regulatory Commission	ROA	return on assets
DTDi	Double Tax Deduction for Internationalization	ROE	return on equity
EBITDA	earnings before interest, taxes, depreciation and amortisation	SEBI	Securities and Exchange Board of India
ECB	European Central Bank	SIA	Singapore Airlines
ETF	exchange traded fund	SME	small and medium-sized enterprise
FDI	foreign direct investment	SOE	state-owned enterprise
FRED	Federal Reserve Economic Data	SPO	secondary public offering
FSC	Korea Financial Services Commission	SPV	special purpose vehicle
GDP	gross domestic product	SWF	sovereign wealth fund
HTT	healthcare, technology and telecommunications industries	TRBC	Thomson Reuters Business Classification
IMF	International Monetary Fund	VAT	value added tax

Executive summary

The COVID-19 pandemic has led to significant challenges for the global economy and financial stability. The measures taken by governments to address the health crisis notably disrupted supply chains and changed ways of doing business in many respects. In Asia, thanks to the measures taken by governments, the region's corporate sector started recovering more rapidly from the crisis than in other regions. However, recent lockdowns in parts of the region may increase economic uncertainty for corporations.

Capital markets played an important role in this recovery by providing financing to otherwise viable businesses struggling during the pandemic, and by supporting research and innovation that helped tackle the health crisis. Well-functioning capital markets will continue to play an important part in the recovery, but will require corporate governance frameworks that give investors, executives, corporate directors and stakeholders the tools and incentives needed to perform their roles in a post-COVID-19 environment.

This is particularly important for Asia as Asian listed companies represent over half of the total number of companies listed around the world and one-third of global market capitalisation. Asian markets also host some of the world's largest companies. At the end of 2020, more than half of the world's largest 10 000 listed companies had their headquarters in Asia. Over the last decade, Asian corporations' investment represented over one-third of global corporate investment and this share is set to increase further.

Asian company profitability is relatively weak compared to the rest of the world, and corporate investment mainly focuses on fixed capital rather than research and development.

The surge in Asian companies' corporate investment and revenues has not been matched by growth in profitability. In 2005, Asian non-financial companies needed USD 1.1 of capital to generate USD 1 of revenue; it now takes almost USD 1.6 to generate that same dollar. This, together with a decrease in profit margins, has negatively impacted firms' profitability. Overcapacity in a number of industries and an increase in non-viable firms ("zombie firms") partly explain these developments.

Asian non-financial companies now invest more in fixed capital than companies in any other region. However, the same is not true for investment in research and development (R&D). Asia notably lags behind the rest of the world in terms of R&D investment in industries such as healthcare and technology.

Although listed firms' leverage has not increased significantly, outstanding debt has surged, mainly driven by firms with lower debt servicing capacity. In emerging and developing Asian markets, firms with lower debt servicing capacity owed almost USD 3 trillion in debt at the end of 2020. Importantly, bank lending remains the dominant type of financing used by the non-financial corporate sector in most Asian economies. This increases both the fragility of the corporate sector and its exposure to shocks. The use of corporate bonds and other debt securities is generally not widespread in Asia and has not grown markedly relative to bank financing.

Asian companies are the largest users of public equity markets.

Asian companies account for 46% of all public equity raised globally since 2009, a marked increase from 22% during the 1990s. This growth is mainly the result of a surge in the number of initial public offerings (IPOs) by Chinese companies, which over the last 10 years was six times higher than during the 1990s.

Hong Kong (China), India, Japan and Korea also rank among the top ten IPO markets globally. Importantly, several Asian emerging markets such as Indonesia, Malaysia and Thailand also rank higher in terms of IPOs than most advanced economies. In terms of industries, financial, technology and industrial companies accounted for 54% of the capital raised via IPOs in Asia between 2012 and 2021.

Asian companies have made extensive use of public equity markets in times of crisis. In 2009 alone, already-listed non-financial Asian companies raised USD 141 billion of public equity at a time when bank financing contracted significantly. This pattern repeated itself during the COVID-19 crisis, when listed non-financial companies raised a total of USD 262 billion in 2020 and USD 301 billion in 2021 via secondary public offerings.

Asian equity markets have also played an important role in providing capital to growth companies. All advanced Asian markets have seen an increase in the share of growth company listings in all listings in 2009-21 compared to the 1990s. In these markets, 9 out of 10 IPOs in the past decade were conducted by growth companies. Asia hosted more than 60% of the world's growth company IPOs in the past five years, of which the People's Republic of China (hereafter 'China') and India together represented half.

Asian corporate bond markets have grown significantly during the past two decades.

Aggregate non-financial corporate bond issuance more than quadrupled from an annual average of USD 129 billion between 2000 and 2008 to USD 602 billion between 2009 and 2021, reaching USD 965 billion in 2021. As a result, the total outstanding amount of non-financial corporate bonds issued by Asian companies reached USD 3.8 trillion in 2021, one-fourth of the global amount. The Chinese market has been the main driver of this growth, increasing from less than 1% of the region's total issuance to roughly two-thirds in 2021.

As Asian bond markets have grown, credit quality has decreased from high levels in the early 2000s. The average rating of Asian issues decreased more than two notches between 2000 and 2021. This trend has not been driven by a marked increase in non-investment grade issuance, as it has remained small at 6.0% in 2021 compared to 22.5% globally. Rather, the reduction in average ratings has been driven primarily by a change in the composition of the investment grade category from higher ratings towards lower investment grade ratings. At the end of 2020, bonds in the BBB category – the lowest investment grade category – represented the largest share of investment grade issuance in Asia with 50% of issuances, similar to the global share. It is worth noting than in 2021, the share of BBB rated bonds in Asia dropped to 37%, making A grades the largest category at 46%, while BBB grades grew to 58% globally.

In contrast with global trends, the most important categories of investors in public equity markets in Asia are corporations, the public sector and strategic individuals.

Asian companies significantly influence today's global corporate ownership landscape. More than half of the total number of listed companies globally are listed in Asia, with 30% in advanced Asian markets and 24% in emerging and developing Asian markets. Ownership structures in Asia differ from structures in the rest of the world. Institutional investors, who own 43% of market capitalisation globally, making them the most important category of investors, own only 18% of the listed equity in Asia. In Asia, corporations, the public sector and strategic individuals are the most important investors in equity markets, owning respectively 20%, 17% and 14% of the listed equity. Importantly, ownership concentration in Asian listed companies is higher compared to global levels. In almost half of the listed companies in Asia and in 60% of the listed companies in emerging and developing Asia, the three largest shareholders own over 50% of the equity.

Capital markets continued financing companies during the COVID-19 crisis.

At the start of the COVID-19 crisis, public equity markets in Asia came to a halt as in the rest of the world. However, following the second quarter of 2020, Asian companies were able to make extensive use of capital markets, although with substantial differences between industries and markets. The decline in the first quarter was most pronounced in advanced Asia, while emerging and developing Asia was less affected. During the third quarter, non-financial companies in Asia raised USD 136 billion, of which China represented almost 70%. In terms of industries, the basic materials, utilities, energy and consumer cyclicals industries saw the largest contractions in fundraising through public equity markets during the first quarter of 2020, while healthcare, consumer non-cyclicals and telecommunications services industries were able to raise more funds compared to historical levels. In 2021, capital raised in Asia reached record amounts, averaging USD 113 billion in each quarter.

In March 2020, many companies resorted to corporate bond markets to alleviate liquidity challenges or to build cushions for future economic uncertainty. In April 2020, Asian corporate bond issuances peaked at USD 105 billion, of which almost 74% was issued by companies from China, while only 6% was issued by companies from other jurisdictions in emerging and developing Asia. In 2020, corporate bonds issued by Chinese, Japanese and Korean non-financial companies together accounted for nearly 90% of all Asian issuances, significantly higher than in previous years. In 2021, in contrast with the decreasing global trend, Asian non-financial companies increased their use of corporate bonds. Issuances by non-investment grade companies, which faced difficulties in accessing bond markets in 2020, reverted to historical levels in 2021.

In response to the COVID-19 crisis, Asian economies adopted a range of measures, spanning from regulatory adjustments to both direct and indirect financial support.

The COVID-19 crisis has put many companies, and indeed entire industries, under severe pressure. To help companies navigate the crisis, all economies adopted a range of measures which have underpinned the recovery. While some of these measures were temporary in nature and introduced for the purpose of mitigating the immediate impact of the crisis, other measures may have a long-term impact on how companies are governed, on their capital and ownership structures, and on how they manage their relationships with shareholders and stakeholders.

The most frequently used direct support measures were loans and loan guarantees. Asian governments also made widespread use of subsidies, grants and capital injections. Many also implemented targeted industry measures, including for the aviation and tourism sectors, and some set up special business funds. Certain governments also used relief packages to promote environmental and digitalisation objectives. The majority of indirect measures aimed to alleviate corporate liquidity needs, including by providing payment deferrals for tax obligations or simply lowering tax ratios, such as corporate income tax. Many economies also waived, lowered or deferred social security contributions, and a large number provided wage and utility subsidies. Regulatory adjustments included, among others, changes to rules for annual general meetings and financial disclosure, measures to facilitate access to capital markets and the tightening of FDI screening mechanisms.

The COVID-19 crisis has highlighted weaknesses in the corporate sector globally, which call for improvements in corporate governance and capital market policies. Against this background, OECD and G20 members are reviewing the G20/OECD Principles of Corporate Governance, taking into account the lessons learnt from the crisis with regard to corporate governance and capital markets. The findings in this report also inform the review process.

1 Corporate landscape

This chapter first provides an overview of the Asian non-financial corporate sector in the last two decades. Using firm-level data, it offers an analysis of trends in financing structure, performance, investment activity and payout policies. It then provides long-term trends on how Asian corporations have used market-based financing by issuing equity and corporate bonds. Finally, the chapter examines the ownership structure of listed companies in the region, identifying the main investor categories and how they invest. These long-term trends provide a starting point for understanding the effects of the pandemic and the challenges ahead.

1.1. Corporate sector overview: Capital structure, performance and investment

The non-financial corporate sector plays a major role in the economy. Although listed non-financial companies represent only a small fraction of the total number of companies globally, they are significant players in the world economy. Their market capitalisation reached USD 87.7 trillion (United States dollar) by the end of 2020, equivalent to total world GDP (Table 1.1). In particular, the number of non-financial listed companies in Asia has grown dramatically in recent years, from 11 649 companies in 2005 to 18 366 in 2020, representing over half of the total number of non-financial listed companies around the world and almost one-third of the total market capitalisation. The growth of Asian economies has been largely driven by the non-financial sector and fuelled by a large wave of investment flowing into the region in recent years. Between 2011 and 2020, Asia attracted over one-third of global foreign direct investment (UNCTAD, 2021[1]).

Using standardised financial information for listed companies, the following section provides a comparative analysis using some key indicators. To provide an overall comparative analysis, it uses financial information from approximately 31 000 non-financial listed companies from around the world.

Table 1.1. Non-financial listed companies as of end-2020

	Market capitalisation (USD trillion)	Leverage	ROE	ROA	Turnover	Investment ratio	Number of companies
World	87.7	31.6%	5.7%	2.2%	58.2%	5.2%	30 914
Asia	27.9	29.2%	5.8%	2.6%	61.1%	5.4%	18 366
China	13.8	28.3%	6.3%	2.8%	59.4%	5.8%	4 562
Japan	6.1	29.0%	6.2%	2.6%	65.4%	5.1%	3 528
India	1.9	32.4%	8.9%	3.6%	61.0%	4.6%	2 581
Korea	2.0	27.9%	3.7%	1.9%	63.7%	6.8%	2 221
ASEAN	1.6	37.4%	1.8%	0.8%	51.5%	3.7%	2 988
Rest of Asia	2.5	27.5%	5.7%	2.8%	59.0%	4.8%	2 486

Note: Leverage is measured as total financial debt divided by total assets. Turnover ratio is measured as total sales divided by total assets. Investment ratio is measured as the sum of capital expenditure, and research and development (R&D) expenses over total assets.
Source: OECD Capital Market Series dataset, Thomson Reuters Datastream, see Annex for details.

The aggregate balance sheet of listed companies in Asia has expanded at a stable pace over time, driven by growth in both equity and liabilities. As shown in Panel A of Figure 1.1, at the end of 2020 the aggregate size of Asian listed companies' balance sheets was USD 31.4 trillion. Equity, including retained earnings, represented 45% of total assets, which is slightly lower than the global level of 50% (OECD, 2021[2]). Liabilities, including both financial debt and non-financial debt such as accounts payables, tax payables and others, accounted for 55% of total assets (Figure 1.1 Panel B). The portion of financial debt has been stable over time, representing around 53% of total liabilities. In 2020, listed companies saw an increase in liabilities of USD 1.6 trillion, including an increase of USD 0.84 trillion in financial debt, largely driven by the companies tapping debt markets to resolve liquidity issues resulting from the COVID-19 pandemic.

The significant increase in total assets has not translated into a similar growth in sales and profits. While total assets almost tripled during the 2005-20 period, aggregate sales only doubled (Figure 1.1 Panel C). Indeed, Asian non-financial companies' assets have made up on average 34% of non-financial assets of listed companies globally between 2005 and 2020, while profits only accounted for 29% of the global figure over the same period (Figure 1.1 Panel D). Although there has been a pronounced increase in profits, particularly in 2017, the aggregate profit in 2020 was around USD 0.8 trillion, which is only 17% higher than in 2007. It is worth mentioning that due to the effective containment measures, in Asia the COVID-19 crisis has not led to significant declines in sales and profits. From a global perspective, in 2020, Asian non-financial companies' share in global profits was 45%, showing strong signs of recovery while the rest of the world was still struggling with the disruptions caused by the pandemic.

Figure 1.1. Overview of non-financial listed companies in Asia

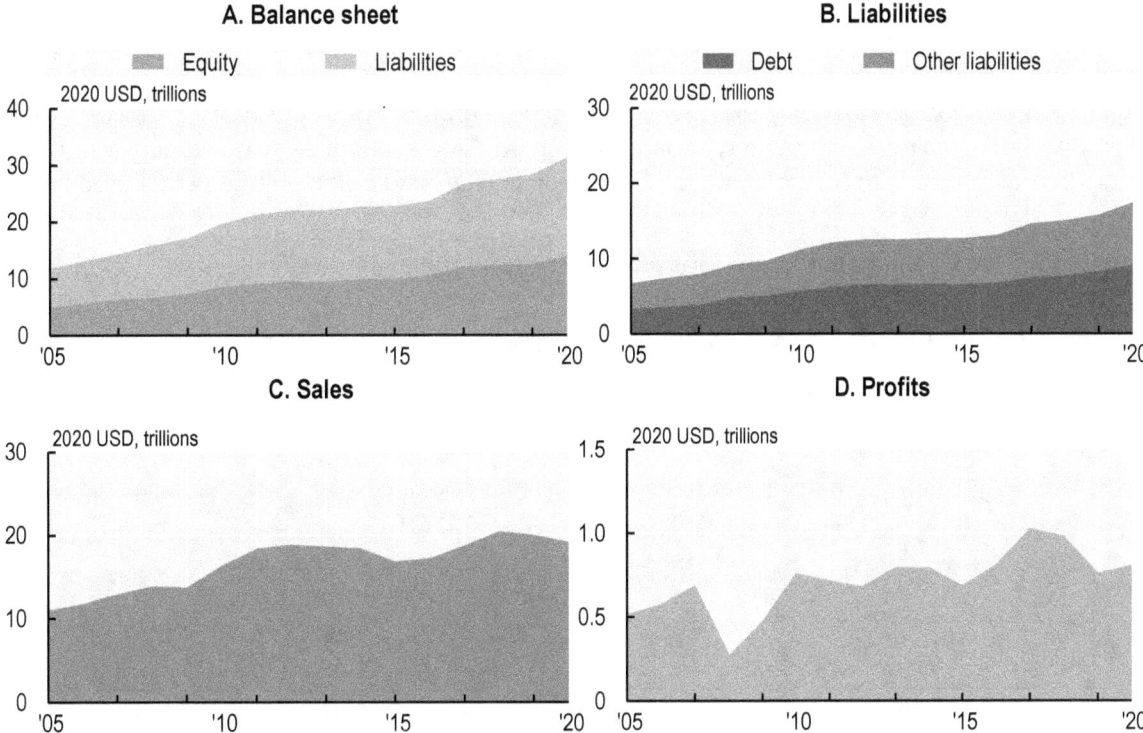

Source: OECD Capital Market Series dataset, Thomson Reuters Datastream, see Annex for details.

The fact that the increase in companies' assets has not been matched by an increase in sales suggests a decline in the operating efficiency of the non-financial corporate sector. For the world excluding Asia, the aggregate assets turnover ratio, measured as sales divided by total assets, decreased from 84% in 2005 to 64% in 2019 and experienced a sharp drop in 2020 to 56% (Figure 1.2 Panel A). Asia is no exception to this trend. Companies in advanced Asia saw their turnover ratios decrease from 96% to 75% over the 2005-19 period, and it dropped further in 2020 to 64%. Similarly, emerging and developing Asian companies' turnover ratios were 81% in 2005, 67% in 2019 and 59% in 2020. Companies in ASEAN economies show a similar trend, with even lower turnover ratios. The assets turnover ratio measures a company's ability to generate sales with its assets and a lower ratio indicates that more assets are required to generate the same level of sales. Growth in total assets does not necessarily lead to growth in sales and profits if investments are not efficient. The recent decrease in operating efficiency could be driven by overcapacity in certain industries, as well as diminishing marginal utility of capital. Meanwhile, the increase in the number of zombie firms, defined as mature companies that are consistently incapable of covering their interest payments with their operating profits, has also led to resources being sunk in unproductive firms, dragging down operating efficiency (Banerjee and Hofmann, 2018[3]). It is also worth mentioning that in advanced Asian markets, non-financial listed companies generally have a higher asset turnover ratio and a lower profit margin compared to emerging and developing Asia (Figure 1.2 Panels A and B). In 2020, as a result of the pandemic, business sales dropped dramatically, leading to a significant decrease in both asset turnover and operating margins.

Driven by the decrease in operating efficiency and profit margin, overall firm profitability has declined over the 2005-20 period. For emerging and developing Asia, the ASEAN economies and the rest of the world excluding Asia, return on assets (ROA) and return on equity (ROE), measures of aggregate profitability, have decreased over the last decade (Figure 1.2 Panels C and D). After a significant decrease during the 2008 financial crisis, both ROA and ROE picked up in 2010. In 2012, with the European sovereign debt crisis, profitability levels dropped substantially again, especially in emerging and developing Asia, as well as ASEAN economies, reaching their lowest levels in 2015 (Lee et al., 2013[4]). After that, profitability started to increase gradually before the pandemic hit. In 2020, firms in most regions experienced a sharp drop in profitability. Outside of Asia, ROA and ROE dropped by 2 and 5 percentage points respectively in 2020, resulting in profitability levels below the ones seen in 2009. Companies in advanced Asia, and emerging and developing Asia only experienced a modest drop in ROA and ROE. However, within the emerging and developing Asia category, companies in ASEAN economies experienced a more severe decrease in profitability, with a 2 percentage points drop in ROA and 5 percentage points drop in ROE.

Figure 1.2. Operating efficiency and profitability of non-financial listed companies

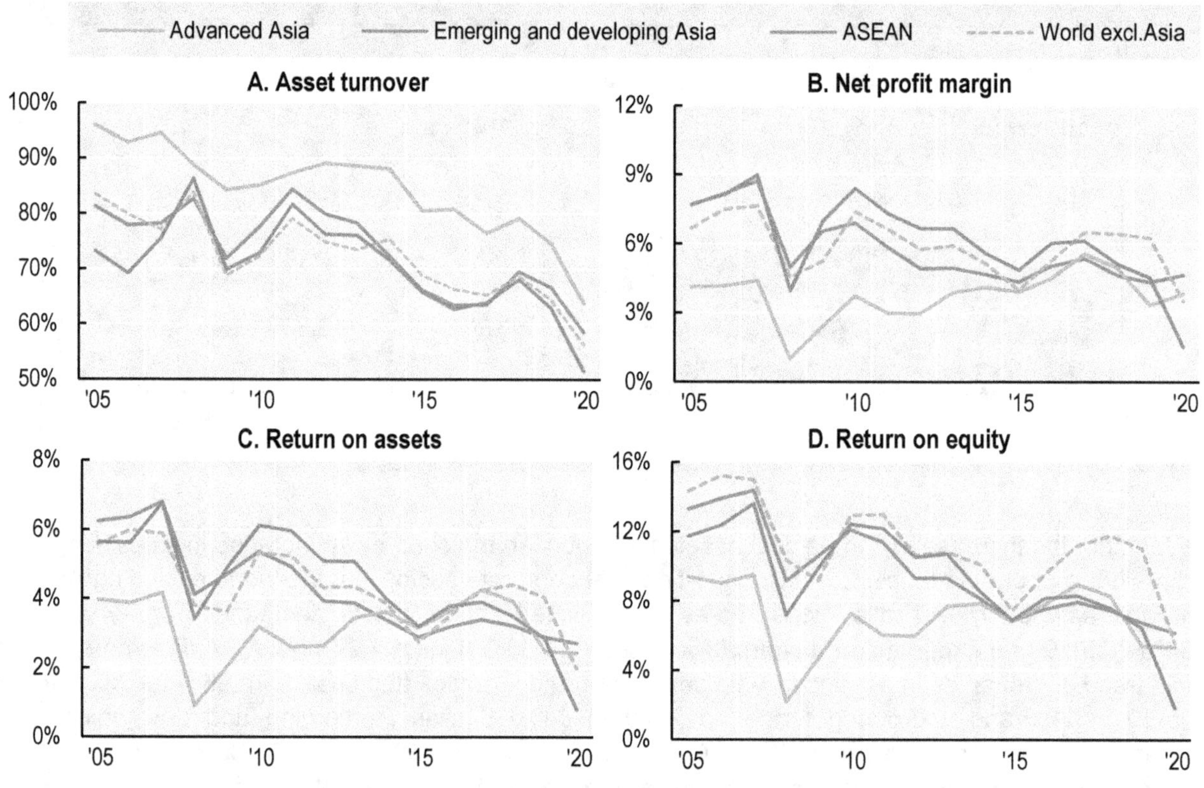

Source: OECD Capital Market Series dataset, Thomson Reuters Datastream, see Annex for details.

Non-financial listed corporations across markets in Asia have witnessed a decline in both asset turnover and profitability over the last two decades (Figure 1.3). In terms of asset turnover, all Asian markets have experienced a drop of 20 to 30 percentage points over the 2005-20 period, indicating lower efficiency. In terms of profitability, China and India have seen significant decreases in profits over time. Meanwhile, corporations in developed markets, such as Japan and Korea, saw a sharp drop in profitability during the 2008 financial crisis. With a gradual recovery in recent years, in 2018 both countries reached their highest profitability levels. However, in 2019, with the prolonged trade frictions between the United States and China, listed firms in Korea and Japan suffered a sharp drop in profit levels. The effect was particularly strong in Korea, a highly export-dependent economy, where the corporate sector experienced a drop of 4 percentage points in ROA. In 2020, despite the COVID-19 pandemic, listed companies in the countries shown in Figure 1.3 performed relatively well. Since the impact of the pandemic was mostly concentrated in firms in more contact-intensive services, which are mostly unlisted, listed companies were less affected by the pandemic. Particularly, Indian non-financial listed companies saw a significant increase in profits, partially driven by a steep cut in corporate taxes from 35% to 26%, as well as cost cutting during the pandemic. Indeed, many firms deferred capital expenditure and internal cash flows were used to reduce debt (Fortune India, 2021[5]).

Figure 1.3. Profitability of non-financial listed companies from selected Asian economies

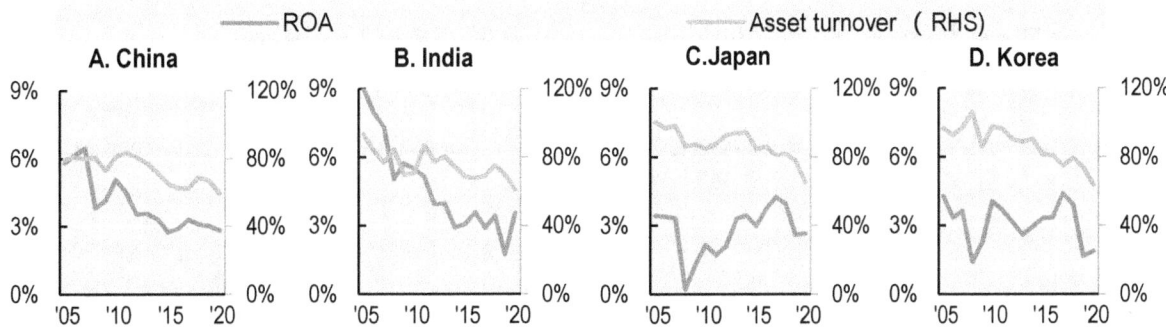

Source: OECD Capital Market Series dataset, Thomson Reuters Datastream, see Annex for details.

A closer look shows a large difference in the distribution of profitability between Asia and the rest of the world over the 2005-20 period (Figure 1.4). Both regions have around 60% to 70% of firms reporting profits below 5% or losses. However, a more detailed composition shows a completely different picture. In Asia, around 40% of firms fall into the profitability range of 0-5%, and 25% of firms make no profits. In the rest of the world, these figures stand at 30% and 40%, respectively. Despite this, the share of companies reporting negative ROA increased from 19% in 2005 to 26% in 2019 and 28% in 2020.

Figure 1.4. Distribution of ROA of non-financial listed companies

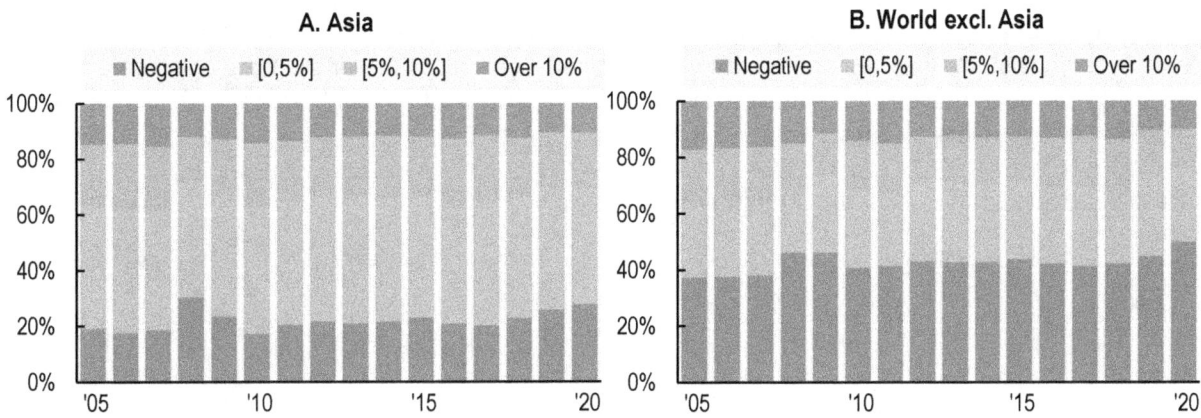

Source: OECD Capital Market Series dataset, Thomson Reuters Datastream, see Annex for details.

The declining trend in profitability has been driven to some extent by a decrease in the share of high-profitability firms. As shown in Figure 1.4, in Asia the share of firms with ROA over 10% among all non-financial listed companies has dropped from 15% in 2007 to 11% in 2020. In the world excluding Asia, this drop is even more significant. After a drastic decrease in profitability following the 2008 financial crisis, the share of high-profitability firms dropped from 16% to 12%. In the following years, despite the recovery, this share fluctuated around 13%, and then dropped to 10% in 2020. During the same period, the share of companies reporting negative ROA went from 37% in 2005 to 45% in 2019 and 50% in 2020.

This decline in the share of high-profitability firms can also be seen when measuring ROE (Figure 1.5). Outside Asia, the share of firms with ROE over 20% dropped from 16% in 2005 to 11% in 2020. For emerging and developing Asia, this drop is even more substantial, with the share of firms with ROE over 20% dropping from almost 20% in 2007 to 8% in 2020. The drop of high-profitability firms in ASEAN economies is also significant, as the total share of firms with ROE over 10% dropped from 38% to 24%.

Figure 1.5. Share of high-profitability non-financial listed companies by ROE

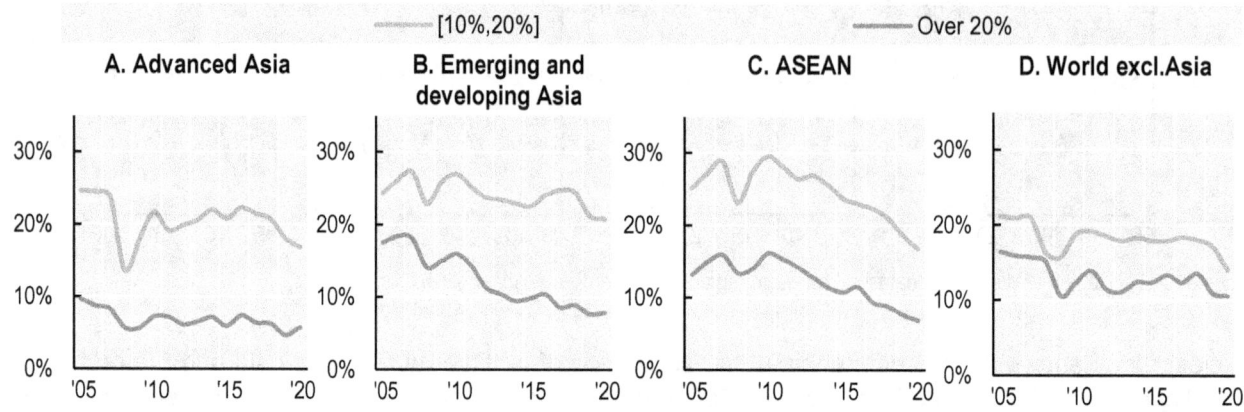

Source: OECD Capital Market Series dataset, Thomson Reuters Datastream, see Annex for details.

The financing structure of non-financial companies in Asia differs slightly from the structure in the rest of the world. Leverage, measured by financial debt over total assets, has been increasing in the rest of the world while in advanced Asia it has remained more or less stable over the period from 2005 to 2020 (Figure 1.6). In emerging and developing Asia, companies' leverage increased gradually from 28% in 2007 to 32% in 2012 before a moderate drop to 30% by the end of 2020. In ASEAN economies, leverage has been on an increasing trend, reaching 37% in 2020, almost 10 percentage points higher than in 2007. A closer look shows that the median leverage has actually been much lower than the aggregate number, indicating that larger firms tend to be the ones with higher leverage ratios and that they are the ones driving the increase in aggregate leverage.

Figure 1.6. Leverage of non-financial listed companies

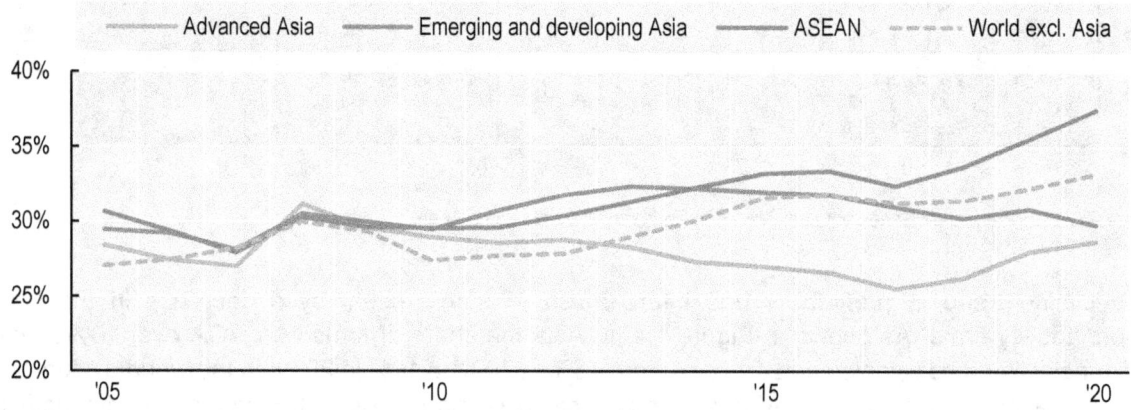

Note: Leverage is measured as total financial debt divided by total assets.
Source: OECD Capital Market Series dataset, Thomson Reuters Datastream, see Annex for details.

As illustrated in Figure 1.7, the distribution of leverage has been consistent over time in advanced Asia, while in emerging and developing Asia, it has changed over time. For emerging and developing Asia, the share of firms with leverage below 10% has increased from 25% to 35% during the period 2005-20, while firms with leverage over 20% decreased from 61% to 47%. By the end of 2020, both emerging and advanced Asian corporations showed similar leverage distributions, where around 10% of firms have a leverage ratio over 50%, with another 37% falling into the range of 20% to 50%. In ASEAN economies, despite the persistent increase in aggregate leverage observed in Figure 1.6, the leverage distribution has not changed significantly over time.

Figure 1.7. Distribution of leverage of non-financial listed companies

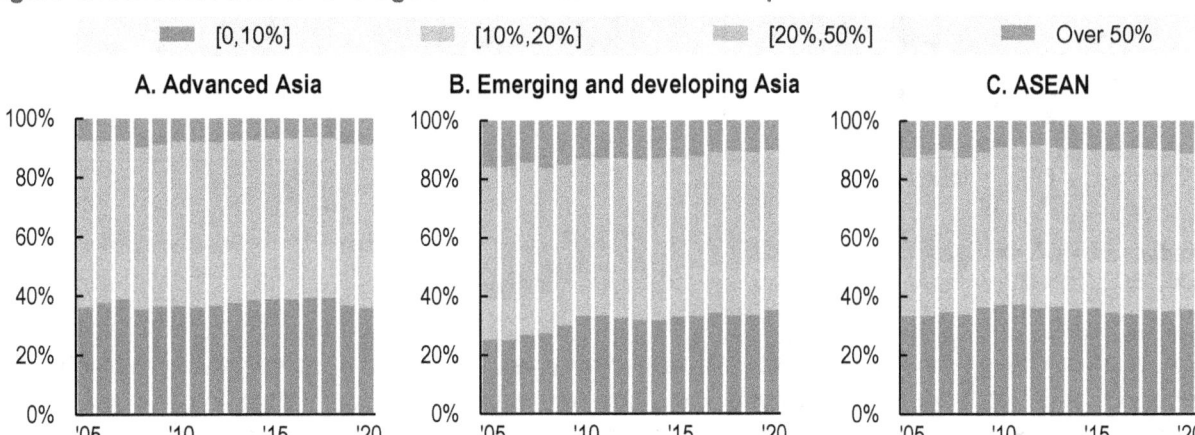

Note: Leverage is measured as total financial debt divided by total assets.
Source: OECD Capital Market Series dataset, Thomson Reuters Datastream, see Annex for details.

Another common leverage indicator used to analyse companies' ability to serve their financial debt and other commitments is the debt-to-EBITDA ratio, which measures a company's indebtedness level against its revenue generation capacity, providing a proxy for the repayment capacity and debt sustainability of the borrower. A higher value reflects a lower capacity to service debt, and this measure is often used as financial covenants in loan contracts (Denis, 2014[6]). In 2005, the aggregate debt-to-EBITDA ratio was 2.4x for corporations in advanced Asia and 2.0x for those in emerging and developing Asia (Figure 1.8 Panel A). This ratio has been on the rise, and in 2019, it stood at 3.3x for corporations in advanced Asia and 3.4x for corporations in emerging Asia. The COVID-19 crisis further drove down firm profits, increasing the respective debt-to-EBITDA ratios to 3.8x and 3.6x.

One important observation is that the share of companies in the higher risk category with respect to their ability to service their debt has increased significantly in the rest of the world, but not in Asia. In fact, during the 2005-20 period, the share of firms with debt-to-EBITDA ratios over 4x increased from 12% to 21% for the rest of world, while in both advanced and emerging Asia it has fluctuated around 25% (Figure 1.8 Panel B). However, in the listed corporate sector in ASEAN economies this ratio has been increasing consistently from 18% in 2010 to 27% in 2020. Moreover, consistent with the distribution of profitability shown in Figure 1.4, Asian companies have a smaller share of companies with negative profits compared to companies outside Asia (Figure 1.8 Panel C).

Figure 1.8. Debt-to-EBITDA ratio of non-financial listed companies

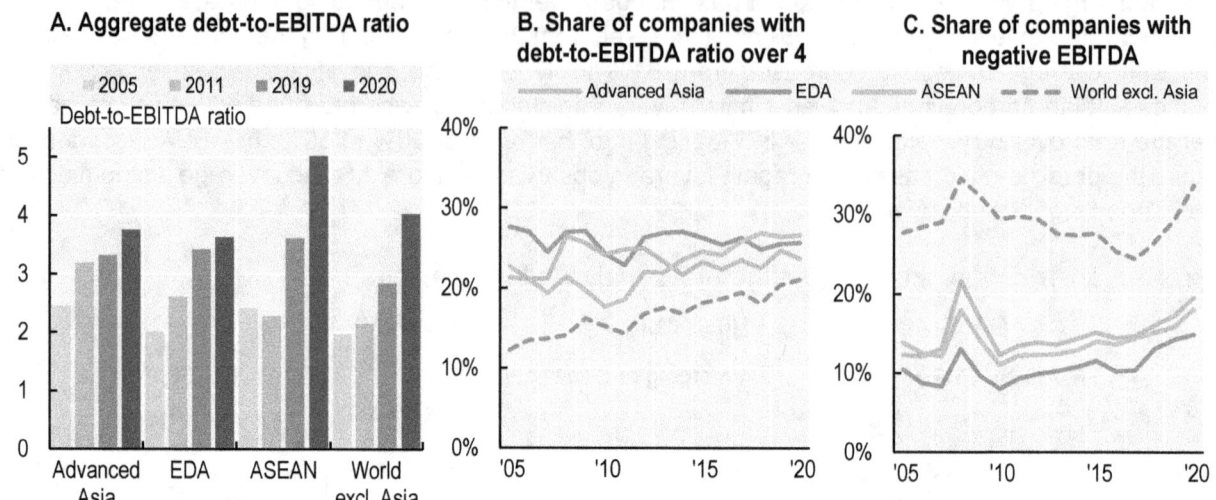

Note: EDA stands for Emerging and developing Asia.
Source: OECD Capital Market Series dataset, Thomson Reuters Datastream, see Annex for details.

However, even though Asia has not seen the same increase in the share of companies in the higher risk category as other regions around the world, there has been an accumulation of debt, in particular by firms with lower debt servicing capacity and in emerging and developing Asia. In fact, in emerging and developing Asia, the total nominal debt owed by firms with debt-to-EBITDA ratio over 4x increased from USD 0.3 trillion in 2005 to USD 2.7 trillion in 2019, and the pandemic has further increased this total to USD 2.9 trillion in 2020 (Figure 1.9). In ASEAN economies, this number has significantly increased from USD 0.1 trillion to USD 0.5 trillion. This development is similar to the rest of the world, where the debt held by firms with lower debt servicing capacity rose from USD 2.8 trillion to USD 6.8 trillion during the 2005-19 period, and further to USD 8.3 trillion by the end of 2020. In advanced Asia, the debt accumulated in the higher risk category has been stable over time, and only surged during the 2008 global financial crisis and in 2019 when the listed companies in Japan and Korea experienced a sharp fall in profits.

Figure 1.9. Debt level of non-financial listed companies by debt-to-EBITDA ratios

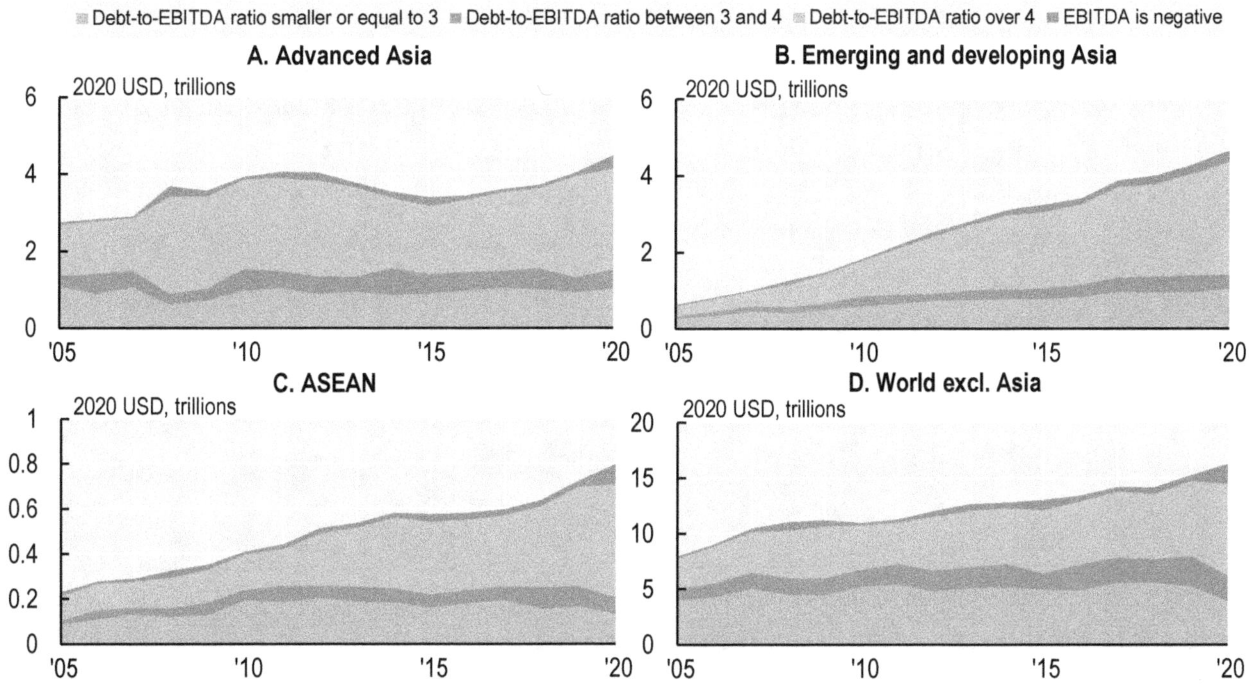

Debt-to-EBITDA ratio smaller or equal to 3 ■ Debt-to-EBITDA ratio between 3 and 4 ■ Debt-to-EBITDA ratio over 4 ■ EBITDA is negative

A. Advanced Asia

B. Emerging and developing Asia

C. ASEAN

D. World excl. Asia

Source: OECD Capital Market Series dataset, Thomson Reuters Datastream, see Annex for details.

When looking at leverage at the economy level, measured as the debt-to-assets ratio of listed corporations, only a few economies have seen significant increases since 2005 (Figure 1.10 Panel A). The most pronounced increase is observed in Singapore and the Philippines, where leverage rose by 12 and 7 percentage points respectively between 2005 and 2020. Indian corporations' aggregate leverage ratio increased from 27% in 2005 to 36% in 2019, a number which dropped to 32% in 2020. In 2020 many firms used internal cash flows to cut debt as capital expenditure was deferred (Fortune India, 2021[5]). A larger increase in leverage is observed when looking at the debt-to-EBITDA ratio (Figure 1.10 Panel B). Indeed, most economies in Asia have seen an increase from around 2x to 3x during the period from 2005 to 2020. Specifically, corporations in Singapore experienced an increase in this ratio from 2.0x in 2005 to 5.1x in 2019, and 6.9x in 2020. In the Philippines, this number increased from 2.4x in 2005 to 4.1x in 2019 and further to 6.0x in 2020.

Figure 1.10. Debt ratio of non-financial listed companies by economy

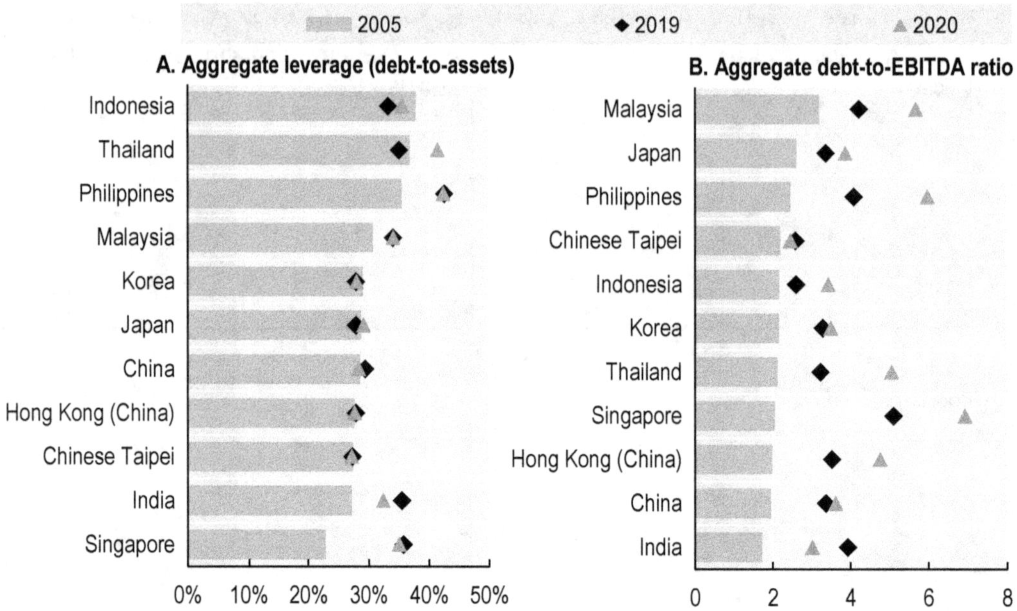

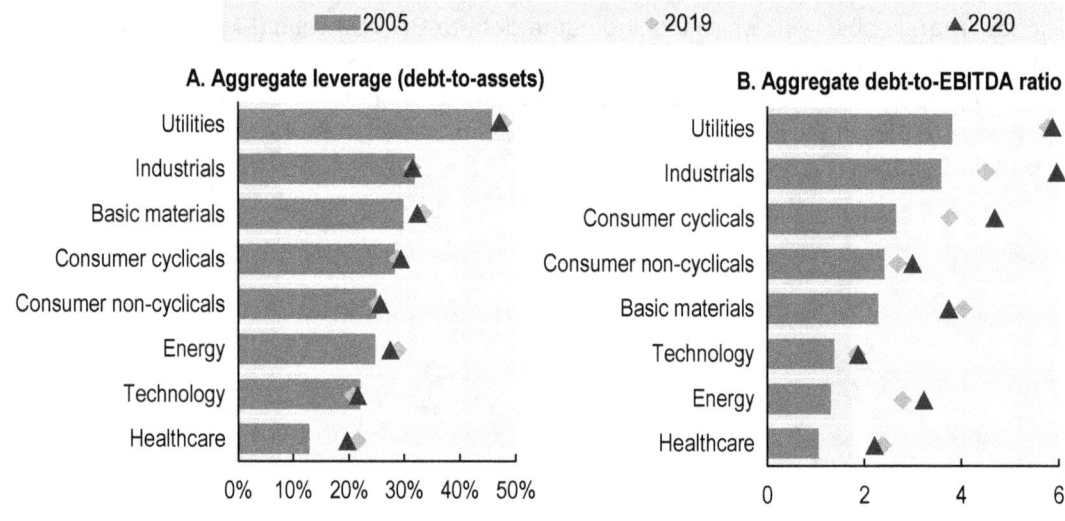

Source: OECD Capital Market Series dataset, Thomson Reuters Datastream, see Annex for details.

As shown in Figure 1.11, although the leverage ratio measured by debt-to-assets has not increased significantly across industries, except for healthcare, almost all industries have experienced a large increase in the debt-to-EBITDA ratio. Industries including basic materials, energy, healthcare and utilities have experienced a pronounced increase in the debt-to-EBITDA ratio in the 2005-20 period. In particular, the aggregate debt-to-EBITDA ratio for utilities surged from 3.8x in 2005 to 5.9x in 2020.

Figure 1.11. Debt ratio of non-financial listed companies in Asia by industries

Source: OECD Capital Market Series dataset, Thomson Reuters Datastream, see Annex for details.

Increasing debt levels and a persistent decline in firms' profitability have led to the rise of zombie companies around the world. These non-viable zombie firms are defined as mature firms that are consistently incapable of covering their interest payments with their operating profits (Adalet McGowan,

Andrews and Millot, 2017[7]).[1] In Asia, the share of zombie companies has also increased and this rise is especially prominent in Singapore, Korea, Malaysia, Indonesia and India (Figure 1.12 Panel A). In these economies, the average share of zombie companies between 2018 and 2020 has stood at around 12%, which is an increase of approximately 5 percentage points from the average between year 2010 and 2012. In Hong Kong (China) the ratio of zombie companies has been consistently high, with on average over 14% of companies identified as zombie companies between 2018-20. These companies also make up a significant share of the total debt of listed corporations. In India, the share of debt in zombie companies' balance sheets increased significantly and reached almost 20% of total listed companies' debt between 2018 and 2020 (Figure 1.12 Panel B). In Indonesia, Singapore, Korea and Hong Kong (China), zombie companies represent around 5% of total debt. The presence of such non-viable companies is a sign of resource misallocation in the economy, and could deprive promising companies of financing opportunities and deter new entrants in the market.

Figure 1.12. Zombie companies by economy / region

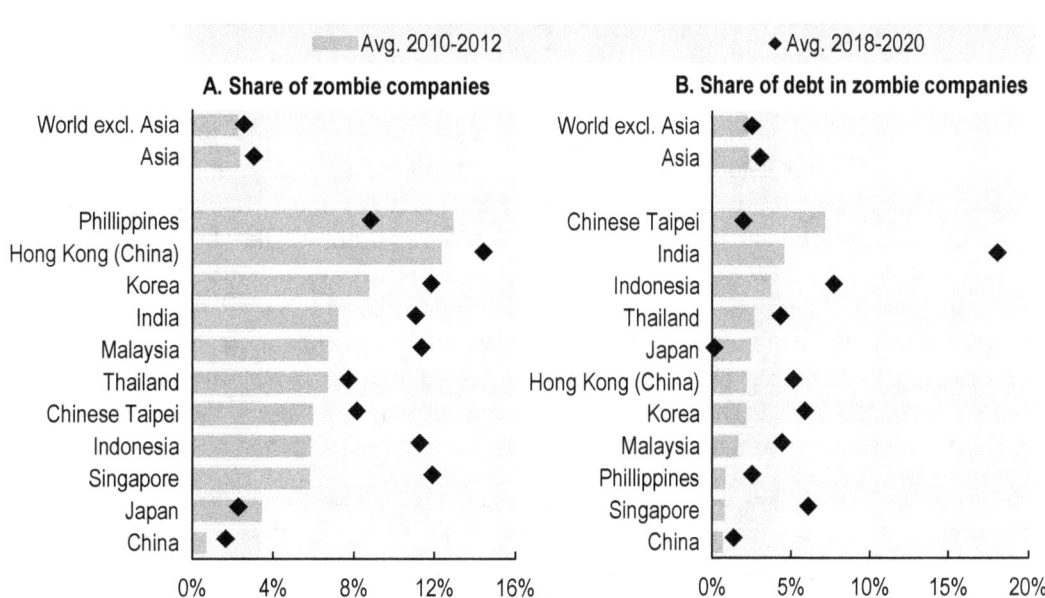

Source: OECD Capital Market Series dataset, Thomson Reuters Datastream, see Annex for details.

Non-financial corporations represent a significant share of total investment globally, and listed companies are responsible for 40% of the non-financial corporate sector's total gross fixed capital formation in OECD countries (OECD, 2021[2]). However, during the last decade, non-financial corporations' investment activity has been sluggish, and Asia has not been the exception to this trend. Indeed, globally, capital expenditure over assets (capex ratio) dropped from 6.0% in 2005 to 4.6% in 2019, and the pandemic drove this ratio further down to 3.8% in 2020 (Figure 1.13 Panel A). In Asia, this number decreased from 6.8% to 4.1% over the 2005-20 period. Similar trends can also be observed in Europe and the United States, with both regions experiencing declines in capital expenditure. It is worth noting that the corporate sector in Asia has been investing more in capex compared to Europe and the United States. The average capex ratio in Asia during the period 2005-20 was 5.7%, compared to 4.8% in Europe and 5.0% in the United States.

Globally, the growth in investment in research and development (R&D) has been mainly driven by the corporate sector in the United States. The R&D ratio, measured by R&D over total assets, has risen from 2.6% in 2005 to 4.5% in 2020 in the United States (Figure 1.13 Panel B). This rise continued despite the pandemic. Meanwhile, in Asia the R&D investment ratio has fluctuated around 1.8% over the same period.

In Europe, the ratio has decreased in recent years, dropping from 2.3% in 2014 to 1.8% in 2020. Importantly, the R&D ratio during the 2005-20 period was on average 1.8% in Asia compared to 3.3% in the United States.

Figure 1.13. Corporate investment of non-financial listed companies by region

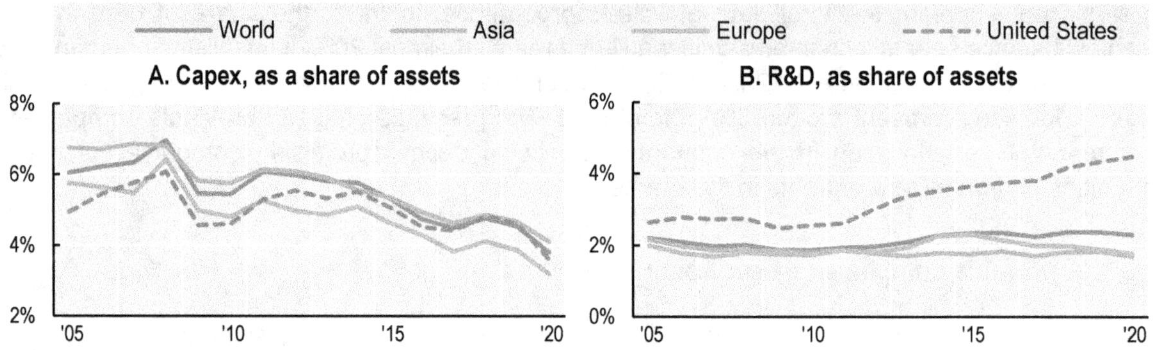

Source: OECD Capital Market Series dataset, Thomson Reuters Datastream, see Annex for details.

Within Asia, capex and R&D of listed non-financial corporations differ significantly across jurisdictions and regions. As shown in Figure 1.14, capex has dropped significantly in almost all regions except Japan. This drop is particularly pronounced in China and India, where capex dropped almost 5 percentage points over the last decade. Korea also saw its capex ratio decrease from 8.4% in 2005 to 4.8% in 2020. On the contrary, the capex ratio in Japanese corporations fluctuated around 5% over the period. There are also significant regional disparities in the intensity of R&D investment. Non-financial listed companies in China and Korea more than doubled their R&D ratios over the period. Indeed, in China it grew from 0.7% to 1.6%, while in Korea it increased from 1.0% to 2.1%. Even though Japan has seen a decline in R&D investments, its average R&D investment over the 2005-20 period is the highest in Asia at 2.3%.

Companies' investment activities also vary significantly depending on the industries they operate in. Energy, technology and utility companies have invested heavily in capex. As shown in Panel A of Figure 1.15, the average capex ratio over the 2011-20 period was 7.4% for Asian listed companies in the energy industry and 6.7% in the technology sector. It is also notable that, except for the energy industry, in almost all industries Asian companies exhibit a higher capex ratio compared to companies in the rest of the world. Regarding R&D investment, the healthcare and technology industries have the highest R&D ratio, followed by consumer cyclicals. Importantly, the corporate sector in Asia still lags behind other regions in R&D investment, especially in the healthcare and technology industries. As shown in Panel B of Figure 1.15, the average R&D ratio for the Asian corporate sector was 5.4% for healthcare and 3.2% for technology, compared to 6.2% and 4.9% respectively for the rest of world.

Figure 1.14. Corporate investment of non-financial listed companies in Asia

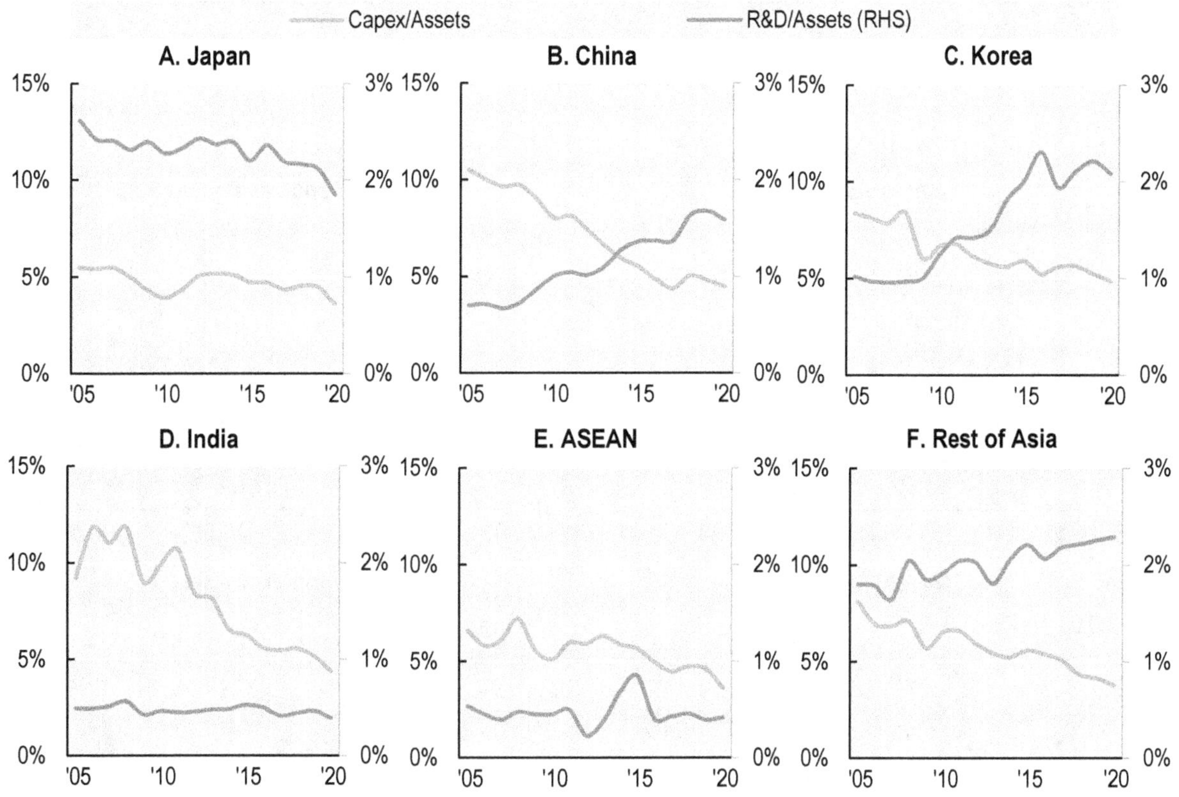

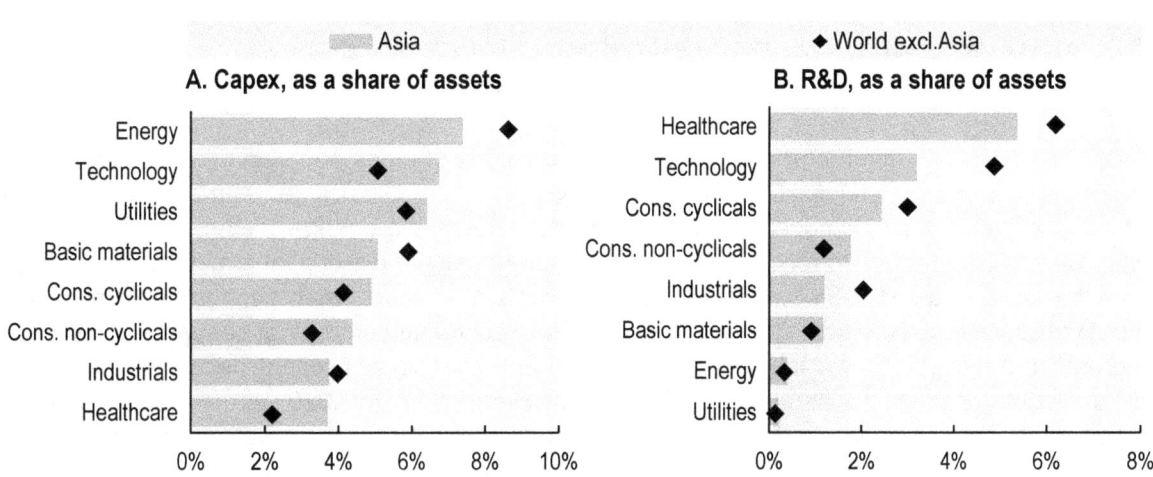

Source: OECD Capital Market Series dataset, Thomson Reuters Datastream, see Annex for details.

Figure 1.15. Corporate investment, average by industry (2011-20)

Source: OECD Capital Market Series dataset, Thomson Reuters Datastream, see Annex for details.

Dividends have grown steadily over the period 2005-20, both in Asia and the rest of the world (Figure 1.16). This trend has been particularly marked for the corporate sector in emerging and developing Asia, where the aggregate amount paid in dividends surged from around USD 44 billion in 2005 to over USD 274 billion in 2020. The dividend payout ratio more than doubled from around 30% during 2005-10 to 60-70% during 2011-20. It is also important to note that during the financial crisis and the COVID-19 pandemic, firms

CORPORATE FINANCE IN ASIA AND THE COVID-19 CRISIS © OECD 2022

continued paying dividends despite declines in earnings or even losses, which had led to a surge in the dividend payout ratio as the denominator, aggregate net income, decreased dramatically during the crisis.

Figure 1.16. Dividends of non-financial listed companies

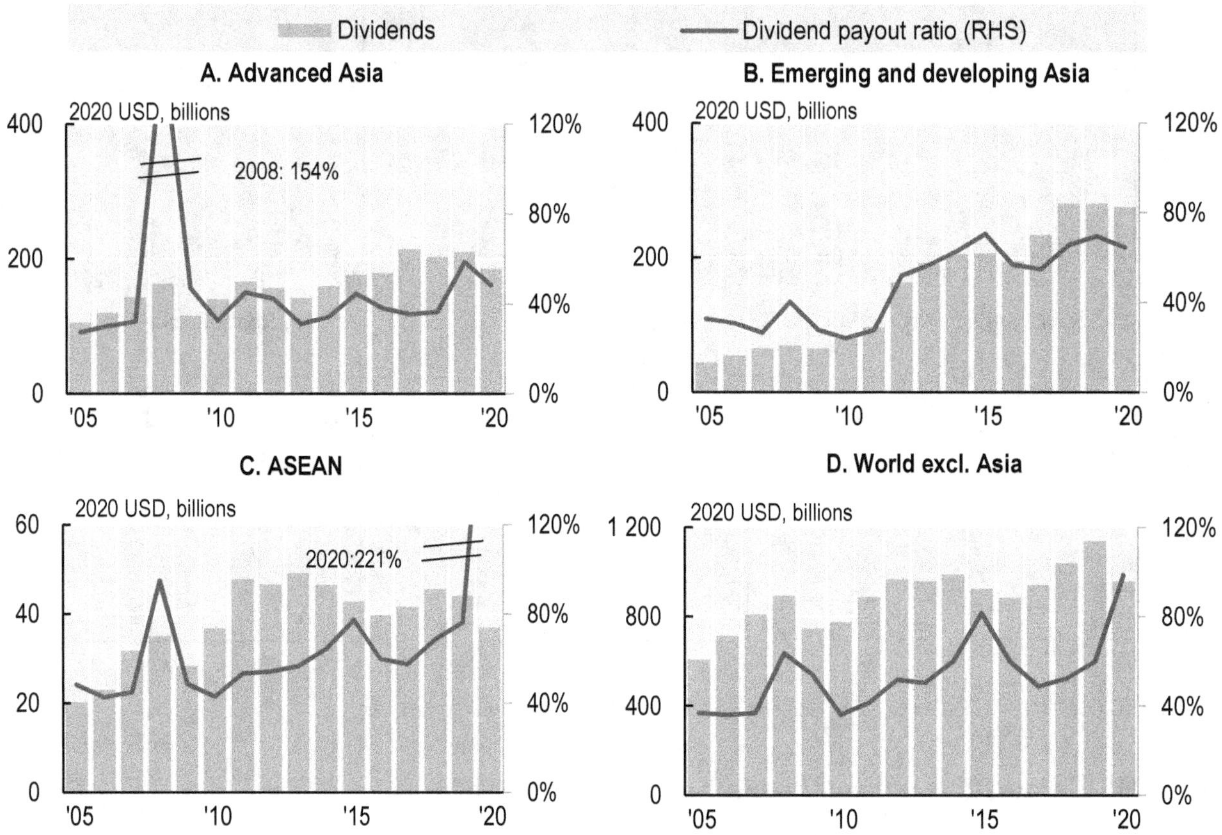
Dividends
Dividend payout ratio (RHS)
A. Advanced Asia
2020 USD, billions
2008: 154%
B. Emerging and developing Asia
2020 USD, billions
C. ASEAN
2020 USD, billions
2020:221%
D. World excl. Asia
2020 USD, billions
'05
'10
'15
'20

Note: Dividend payout ratio is measured as dividends divided by net income before extraordinary items.
Source: OECD Capital Market Series dataset, Thomson Reuters Datastream, see Annex for details.

Corporate debt exists in different forms, consisting of a variety of loans and securities with different cash flow claims and provisions. Due to the different properties of debt instruments, many companies have significantly adjusted their composition of debt without substantial change to their debt levels (Rauh, 2010[8]). Thus, it is important to recognise the debt heterogeneity in the capital structure. Bank lending is the dominant type of credit used by non-financial corporations in most Asian economies. While there are notable exceptions (see Section 1.3), the use of corporate bonds and other debt securities is generally not widespread and has not grown markedly relative to bank financing in recent decades in a number of significant Asian jurisdictions, as shown in Panel A of Figure 1.17. In 2020, the average share of debt securities in financial debt for the four jurisdictions presented in Panel B was 22%. In Korea, the share decreased between 2008 and 2020, whereas it grew marginally in Japan. In India, the use of debt securities grew quite substantially, almost doubling over the period.

These shares are low compared to the United States, where the use of debt securities by non-financial companies is very common, representing 65% of their total financial debt (OECD, 2021[2]). Korea and India are in line with the levels seen in the United Kingdom, where the share was 28% in Q3-2020 (ONS, 2021[9]). Japan is closer to the low levels seen in the Euro Area, where the share was 13% in 2020 (ECB, 2021[10]).

Figure 1.17. Bank lending versus debt securities in selected Asian economies

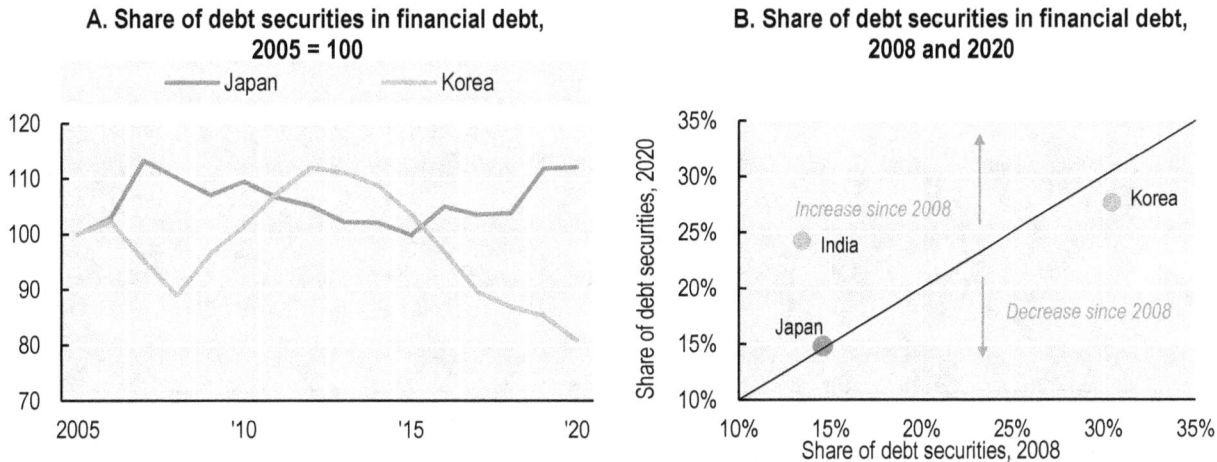

Note: In Panel A, India has been excluded because the available time series starts in 2010. In Panel B, Indian values are from 2019 and 2010, respectively.
Source: Bank of Japan, Bank of Korea, Reserve Bank of India.

Corporate bonds can be an important source of financing for non-financial companies, offering a way to diversify and lengthen the maturity of their borrowing. This is of particular importance in times of crisis, when the availability of bank credit tends to contract. Both in the aftermath of the 2008 financial crisis and during the pandemic-induced crisis of 2020, companies issued significant amounts of debt through corporate bonds in order to meet immediate obligations to stakeholders or to roll over existing debt. An under-developed corporate bond market can result in a lack of balance sheet diversification among companies and an over-dependence on bank lending, which may have broader economic and financial stability implications when credit conditions tighten.

Figure 1.18 offers a closer look at how non-financial companies finance themselves in a number of Asian economies. As is clear from the capitalisation ratio, measured by equity over total assets, shown in Panel A, equity is the single most important source of financing in Japan where non-financial corporations finance their activities with more than 50% of equity. However, the equity levels stand below 50% of total assets in Korea and India. Lower levels of equity in the balance sheet conversely imply a higher share of liabilities. For example, in Korea and India the aggregate share of liabilities on the balance sheet is 52% and 60% respectively. Looking at the composition of total liabilities as presented by Panel B of Figure 1.18, loans, which include loans from non-financial institutions, is the largest component in the liability structure of the non-financial corporate sector. On the contrary, in all jurisdictions, debt securities make up the smallest component of aggregate liabilities. Only Korean companies show relatively widespread use of debt securities in their capital structure.

Figure 1.18. Capital structure of non-financial companies in selected economies as of end-2020

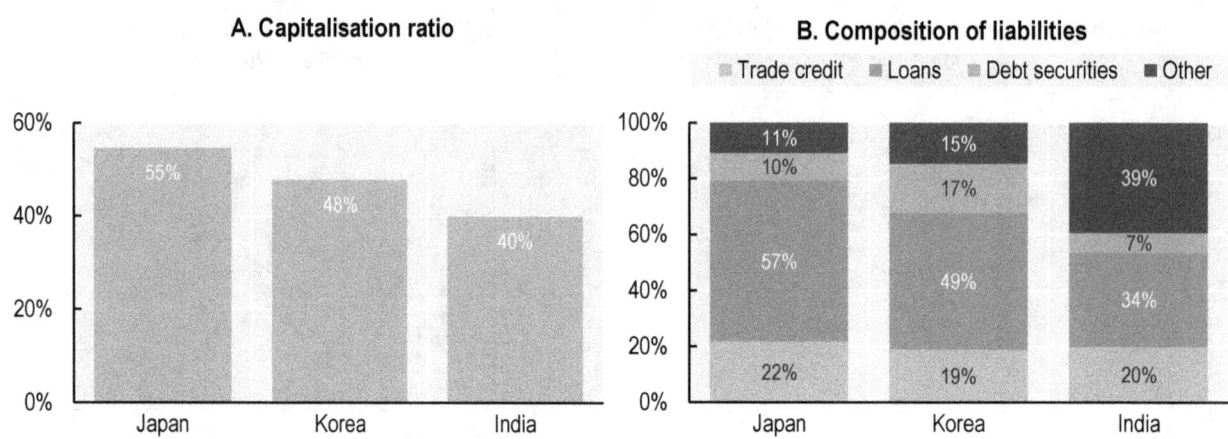

Note: The values in the figure represent aggregate numbers. Indian values are for 2018.
Source: Bank of Japan, Bank of Korea, Reserve Bank of India.

Importantly, the non-performing loans (NPL) ratio in the region more broadly has been stable and relatively low in the past decade, with no notable increase after the 2008 financial crisis (Figure 1.19). This trend holds for both advanced and emerging Asian economies. This is in sharp contrast to the European Union, which is also heavily bank-dependent, where the share of NPLs rose sharply after the financial crisis and remained elevated during the subsequent euro crisis with significant negative impact on economic performance and financial stability.

Figure 1.19. Non-performing loans ratio in selected regions

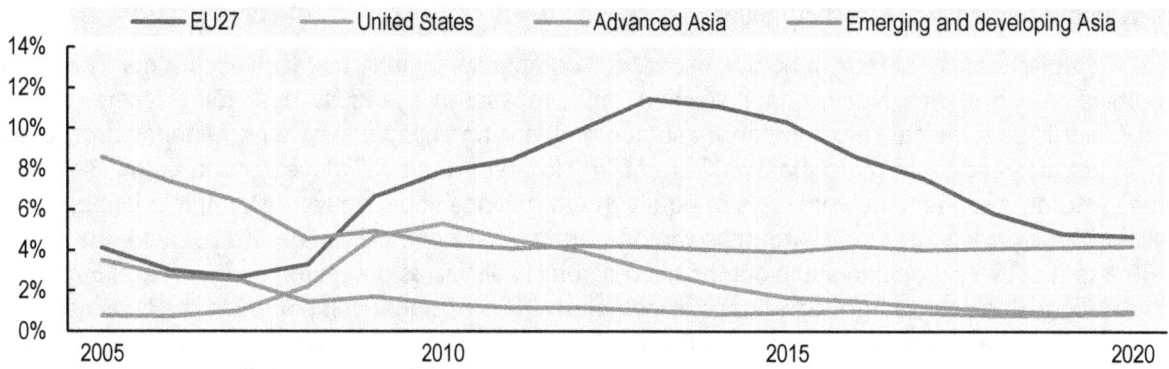

Note: Simple averages. United States data are annual averages based on quarterly figures.
Source: IMF Financial Soundness Indicators, Bank of Japan, Federal Reserve Bank of St. Louis FRED.

However, the aggregate figures conceal significant differences across jurisdictions. As Figure 1.20 shows, the NPL ratio varies widely, from 9.2% in Pakistan to 0.3% in Korea. There are also substantial differences in how the ratio has developed over time. In six out of 15 jurisdictions, the NPL ratio decreased between 2011 and 2020, by an average of 42% (1.9 percentage points). In the remaining nine jurisdictions, it increased by an average of 53% (1.3 percentage points). Three out of six jurisdictions that decreased their ratio between 2011 and 2020 already had a ratio below the median in 2011.

Figure 1.20. Non-performing loans ratio by jurisdiction

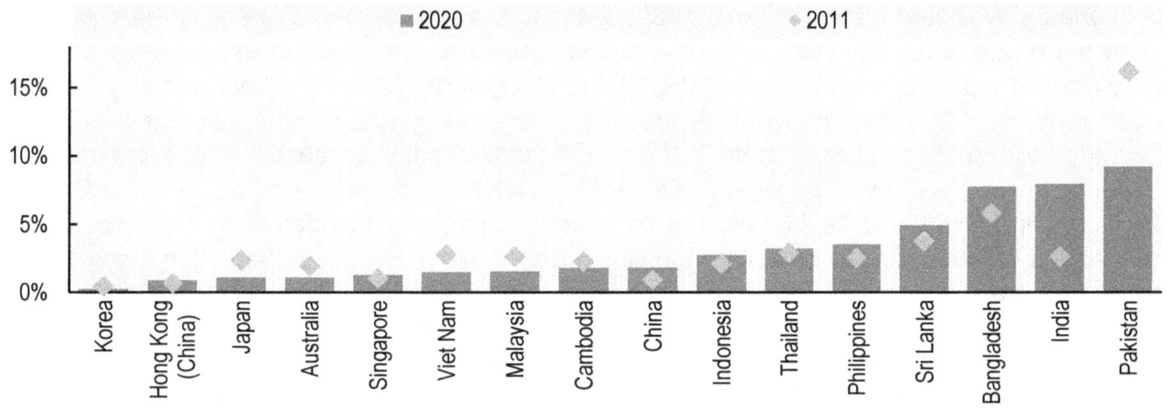

Note: Most recent values for Korea, Singapore and Viet Nam are from 2019.
Source: IMF Financial Soundness Indicators, Bank of Japan.

Substantial levels of NPLs is a symptom of inefficient allocation of capital, as funding is locked into firms that are unable to generate enough profits to repay their debts. Aside from having detrimental effects on the resilience of the banking system, this may act as a constraint to credit access even for viable and productive firms. Such a development is closely associated with the growing phenomenon of "zombie firms", mature companies that are continuously unable to meet their interest payments (OECD, 2021[2]). In order to enable credit to flow to productive firms rather than stay sunk in unproductive ones, it is important that national insolvency systems facilitate procedures to allow fundamentally non-viable firms to exit the market while restructuring the debts of fundamentally viable ones. Failure to do so may lead to extended periods of underinvestment and sluggish economic growth.

1.2. Trends in the use of public equity

Equity capital is by nature a long-term and risk-sharing source of financing for corporations. It gives companies the opportunity to invest in projects with uncertain outcomes such as research, development and innovation that contribute to business dynamism, productivity and economic growth. Moreover, already-listed companies can also continue benefitting from public equity markets by raising additional capital. In this respect, public equity markets are well-suited to increase the resilience of the corporate sector by providing a cushion to companies that need to overcome temporary downturns and at the same time meet their obligations to employees, creditors and suppliers. For instance, in 2009, non-financial listed companies raised a historical record amount of USD 535 billion of new equity through the stock market at a time when bank financing contracted significantly. This pattern repeated itself in 2020 and 2021, when already non-financial listed companies raised a record total of USD 656 billion and USD 645 billion via secondary public offerings, respectively.

The scrutiny of equity markets serves a critical role in efficiently allocating capital to long-term viable businesses rather than companies that have structural weaknesses and limited prospects to survive. Importantly, from the perspective of ordinary households, public equity markets provide them an opportunity to directly or indirectly participate in the corporate value creation and offer additional options for managing savings and retirement plans. With over 40 000 listed companies worldwide totalling a combined market value of about USD 105 trillion, public equity markets remains the largest asset class available to the general public.

1.2.1. Initial public offerings (IPOs) trends

One important development since the mid-1990s is the increased use of public equity markets by Asian companies. Between 2009 and 2021, 46% of all public equity in the world was raised by Asian companies. This is a marked increase from 22% during the 1990s. The growth of Asian markets is mainly the result of a surge in Chinese IPOs. The number of Chinese IPOs more than quadrupled between the 1990s and the post-2008 period, when they represented almost one-third of global proceeds. The Japanese market, which during the 2000-08 period experienced a decline in total IPO proceeds compared to the 1990s, saw a 44% increase during the 2009-21 period, which also contributed to the increased importance of Asian equity markets. While seeing fewer IPOs than China and Japan since 2000, the Indian market has also experienced a gradual increase in the amount of capital raised through IPOs since 1990. In Korea, funds raised have increased slightly over the three periods presented below in Figure 1.21, and Thailand saw a significant increase over the last period compared to the 2000-08 period, mainly driven by the proceeds raised in 2020 and 2021. As a result of the surge in Asian IPOs, the global share of Asian listed companies has also increased. At the beginning of 2021 over half of the world's listed companies were listed on Asian stock exchanges, together representing one-third of the market value of listed companies globally.

Figure 1.21. Initial public offerings, total amount raised

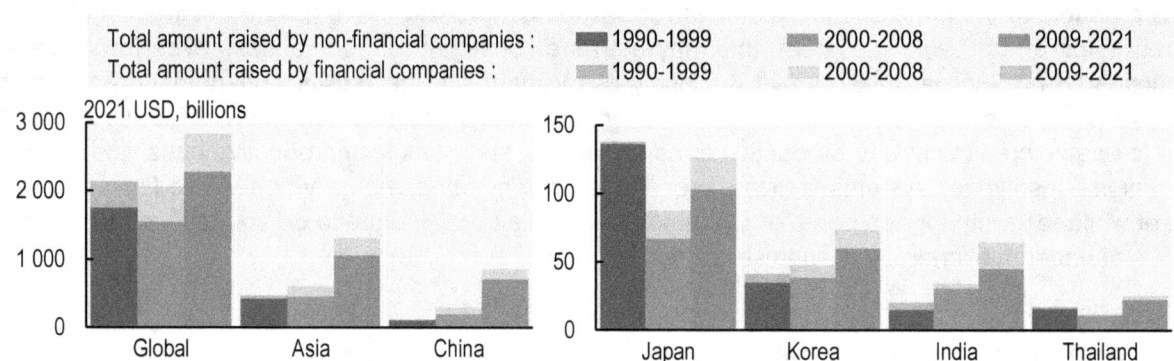

Source: OECD Capital Market Series dataset, see Annex for details.

The shift towards Asia has been even more pronounced with respect to the number of IPOs by non-financial companies. As seen in Figure 1.22, Chinese non-financial companies have been the world's most frequent users of IPOs during the past decade, with twice as many IPOs as in the United States. Moreover, other Asian markets – Hong Kong (China), India, Japan and Korea – also rank among the top ten IPO markets globally. Importantly, several Asian emerging markets, such as Indonesia, Malaysia and Thailand, rank higher in terms of IPOs than most advanced economies. Ten out of the 20 top IPO markets globally between 2012 and 2021 were in Asia.

Figure 1.22. Top 20 jurisdictions by number of non-financial company IPOs between 2012 and 2021

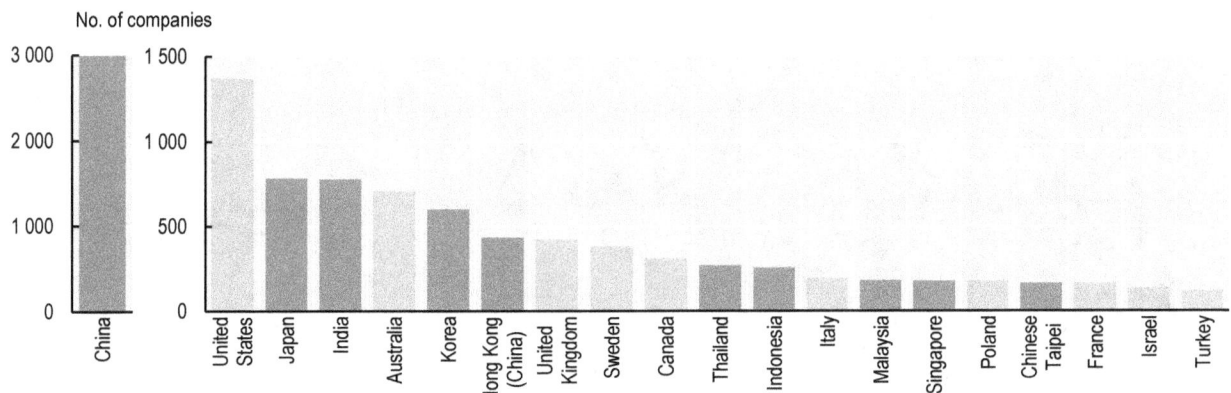

Source: OECD Capital Market Series dataset, see Annex for details.

The change in the global public equity market landscape has not only been driven by a shift in the number of new listings towards Asian markets. Another contributing factor is the increasing number of companies that have delisted from the stock markets. Since 2005, over 33 000 companies have delisted from public stock markets globally (Figure 1.23). Specifically, there were 8 400 delistings of European companies over the 2005-21 period, and 6 000 delistings of US companies. Similarly, in Asia, 6 700 companies delisted, of which around 1 400 were Japanese. In the United States, these delistings were larger than the number of new listings, resulting in a net decrease in the number of listed companies every single year between 2005 and 2020. Notably, in 2021, the trend was reversed with more than 300 new listings against 200 delistings. In Europe, the number of delistings surpassed the new listings every year since 2008. However, in Asia, net listings were positive in every year between 2005 and 2021. In Japan, net listings were positive in 11 out of the 17 years shown. In China, there were on average 36 delistings per year against an average of almost 270 new listings, resulting in a considerable net increase in the total number of listed companies. In Korea, net listings were negative only in 2009, 2010 and 2012.

The growth of Asian stock markets and the growing number of delistings in advanced economies, mostly in the United States and Europe, are not the only important developments inthe global equity markets during the past decade. Another key development is the decline in the listings in some advanced markets of smaller growth companies, defined as those raising less than USD 100 million in an IPO. In the United States, for example, the share of growth company listings in all listings was 45% during the 2009-21 period compared to 77% during the 1995-99 period. The United Kingdom has seen a similar trend, with an average of 73% of growth company listings during 2009-21 against 84% in the first period. However, all advanced Asian markets have all seen an increase in the share of growth company listings in all listings in 2009-21 compared to the 1990s. In these markets, nine out of ten IPOs in the past decade were conducted by growth companies. Notably, Asia has hosted more than 60% of the world's growth company IPOs in the past five years, of which China and India together represented half.

Figure 1.23. Newly listed and delisted companies

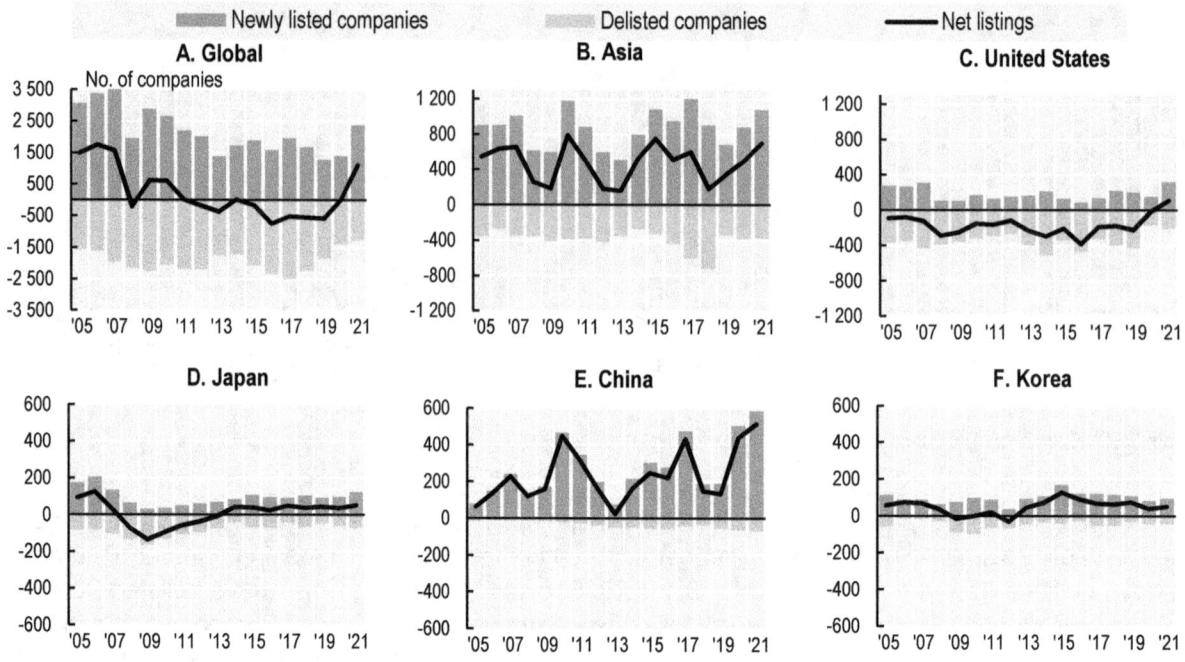

Source: OECD-ORBIS Corporate Finance dataset, OECD Capital Market Series dataset, see Annex for details.

Figure 1.24. Growth company IPOs' share in the total number of non-financial company IPOs

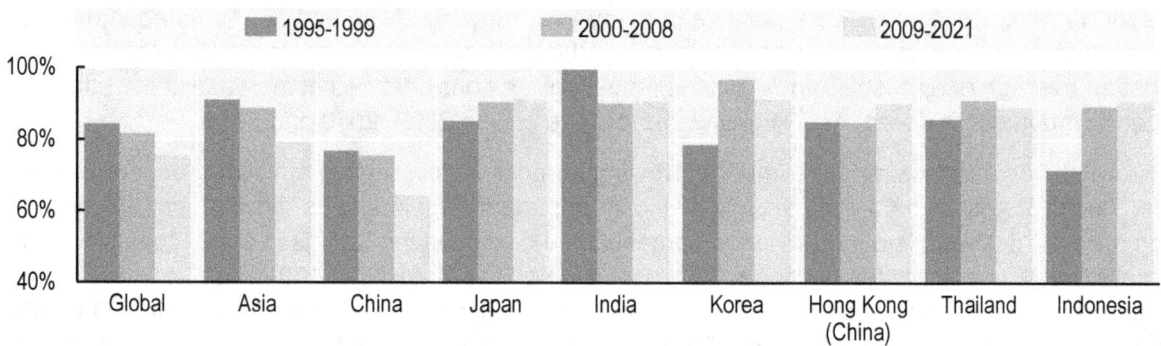

Source: OECD Capital Market Series dataset, see Annex for details.

As the largest users of public equity markets, Asian companies have also become important issuers in non-domestic markets. At the end of 2020, 526 Asian companies were listed on a market different from the one where they were domiciled[2] (Figure 1.25 Panel A). While these companies only accounted for 2% of the total number of listed companies in Asia, they represented one-third of the total non-domestic listed companies globally. In terms of market capitalisation, Asian non-domestic listed companies represent 5.6% of the market capitalisation of the companies domiciled in Asia, slightly over the 5% global share of non-domestic listed companies. Chinese companies represent 90% of the market capitalisation of Asian companies listed on a non-domestic stock exchange. Globally, the United States hosts most of these non-domestic listings with 610 companies, followed by the United Kingdom with 257 companies (Figure 1.25 Panel B). The United States also hosted the highest number of non-domestic listings of Asian companies. In fact, five jurisdictions hosted almost 90% of the non-domestic listings of Asian companies, namely the United States, Hong Kong (China), Singapore, Australia and the United Kingdom (Panel C).

Figure 1.25. Non-domestic listed companies and host stock exchanges' jurisdiction as of end-2020

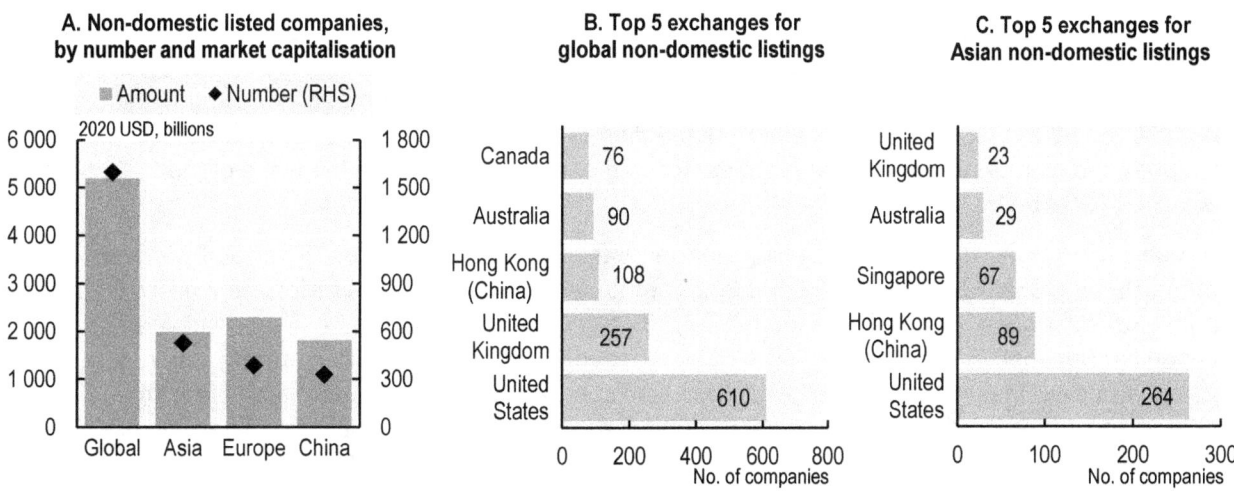

Note: In Panel A, China includes both mainland China and Hong Kong (China).
Source: OECD Capital Market Series dataset, see Annex for details.

A breakdown of the total proceeds from IPOs across different industries between 2012 and 2021 shows that companies in the financial, technology and industrials sectors have absorbed a significant part of both global and Asian IPO proceeds. There are some noteworthy differences in Japan and India compared to the other Asian jurisdictions shown in Figure 1.26. Industrial companies dominate the Japanese IPO market with 29% of all proceeds, while financials correspond to 38% of all proceeds in India.

Figure 1.26. Distribution of IPO proceeds by industry (share in total proceeds, 2012-21)

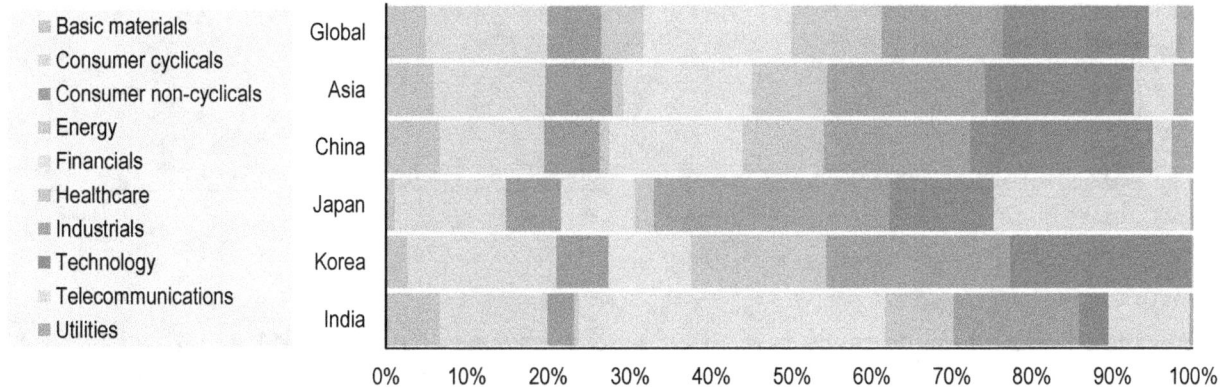

Source: OECD Capital Market Series dataset, see Annex for details.

The healthcare, technology and telecommunications industries (HTT) have a cumulative share of 33% of all global and Asian proceeds. Technology companies are dominant within the HTT industries in most of the Asian jurisdictions provided in Figure 1.26, while the Japanese HTT industries are dominated by the telecommunications industry. Out of the total IPO proceeds that went to the HTT industries in China and Korea, technology accounted for 23% of the total amount raised in both jurisdictions. India differs significantly in terms of the share of HTT industries among the Asian jurisdictions shown in the figure. In India, the share of HTT industries represents only 22%, with technology accounting for no more than 4% of total IPO proceeds.

CORPORATE FINANCE IN ASIA AND THE COVID-19 CRISIS © OECD 2022

1.2.2. Secondary public offerings (IPOs) trends

Secondary public offerings (SPOs) allow companies that are already-listed to continue raising equity capital on primary markets after their IPO. The proceeds from an SPO may be used for a variety of purposes and can also help fundamentally sound companies bridge a temporary downturn, such as the crisis caused by the COVID-19 pandemic. As mentioned in the introduction to this section, SPOs played an important role in providing the corporate sector with equity capital both in the wake of the 2008 financial crisis and in 2020-21.

The use of SPOs as a source of funding has increased in recent decades. The total proceeds raised through SPOs globally between 2009 and 2021 amounted to almost USD 9 trillion, which is 3.6 times the amount raised during the 1990s (Figure 1.27). The global SPO market is also dominated by Asian companies. Between 2009 and 2021, 36% of all proceeds raised through SPOs worldwide were raised by Asian companies. Importantly, the proceeds by Asian companies increased more than eight times between 1990-99 and 2009-21. China represents a significant part of this development. The use of SPOs by Chinese companies was marginal during the 1990s, but since 2009 they have raised USD 1.6 trillion in equity through SPOs, equal to 18% of the global amount over the same period. In Japan, the capital raised via SPOs more than doubled between 1990-99 and 2009-21. Indian, Korean and Thai companies also raised more capital via SPOs in 2009-21 than in the 1990s. In particular, Indian financial companies raised USD 164 billion via SPOs during the 2009-21 period, equivalent to almost one-fifth all capital raised via financial SPOs in Asia.

Figure 1.27. Secondary public offerings, total amount raised

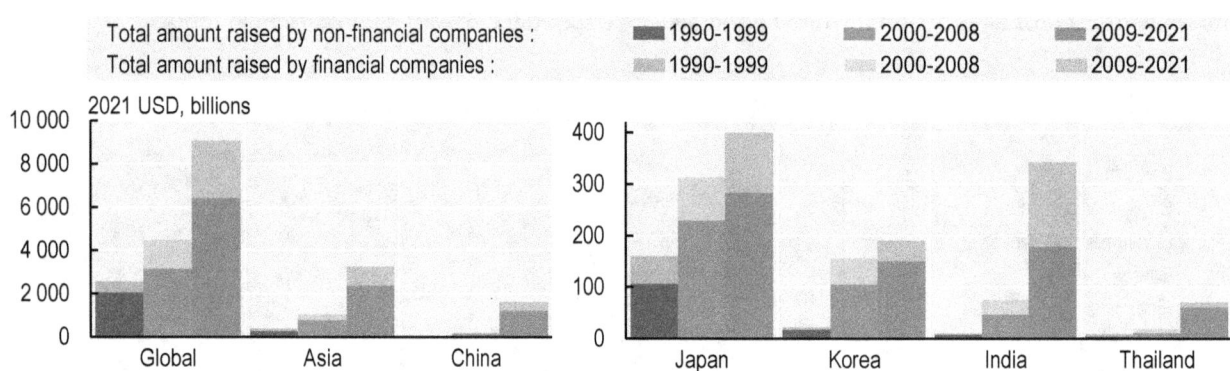

Source: OECD Capital Market Series dataset, see Annex for details.

A breakdown of the total proceeds from SPOs across industries between 2012 and 2021 shows that financials and industrials companies, after raising a significant share of capital in IPOs, continued raising capital via SPOs (Figure 1.28). While companies from the healthcare, technology and telecommunications industries (HTT) also raised considerable amounts of capital via SPOs, their share in total SPOs proceeds was lower than in IPOs proceeds. The HTT industries' share of proceeds for Asia as a whole is 22%, roughly the same as the global figure. Among the Asian jurisdictions presented in the figure, Japan has the highest share of proceeds by HTT industries with 27%, followed by China with 25%. As with IPOs, financial company proceeds accounted for a significant share (53%) of the total Indian SPO proceeds. On the other hand, the HTT industries' share of proceeds was only 14% in India.

Figure 1.28. Distribution of SPO proceeds by industry (share in total proceeds, 2012-21)

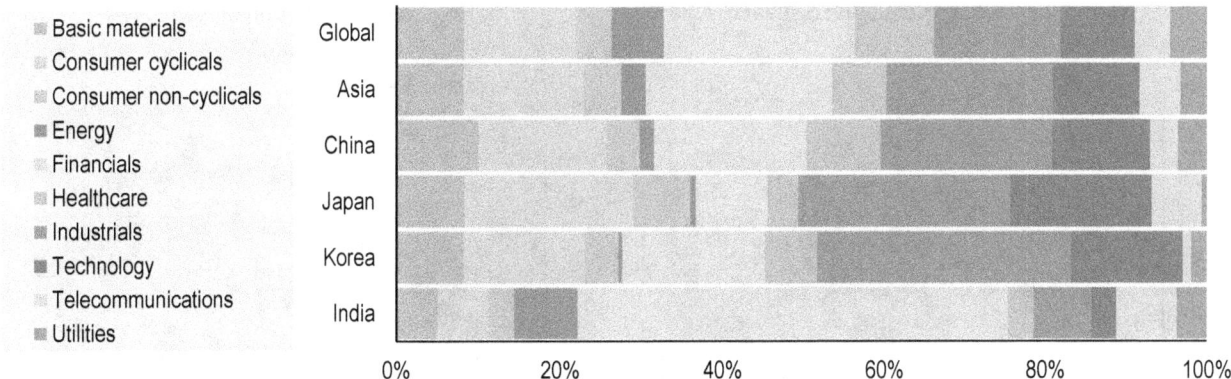

Source: OECD Capital Market Series dataset, see Annex for details.

1.3. Trends in the use of corporate bonds

Corporate bonds have become an increasingly important source of financing for non-financial companies in recent years (Çelik, Demirtaş and Isaksson, 2015[11]). They offer companies a way to diversify their funding and to access long-term financing, as seen in the significant increase in the proportion of corporate bonds with longer maturities in recent years (Badoer, 2016[12]). Since the 2008 financial crisis, there has been a considerable shift from bank loans to bonds (Becker and Ivashina, 2014[13]). Indeed, global bond issuance amounts doubled from an annual average of USD 932 billion before the crisis (between 2000-07) to an annual average of USD 2 trillion in the period between 2008 and 2021. Following the outbreak of the COVID-19 crisis, corporate bonds have represented a significant source of capital for the non-financial corporate sector. In 2020 and 2021, global bond issuances by non-financial companies reached a historical peak of USD 3 trillion and USD 2.5 trillion, respectively, resulting in an all-time high of USD 15.3 trillion in outstanding non-financial corporate bonds at the end of 2021.

Asian corporate bond markets have undergone a complete transformation in the past two decades. Aggregate issuance has grown from a relatively low level of USD 129 billion annually between 2000 and 2008 to USD 602 billion between 2009 and 2021, reaching USD 965 billion in 2021 (Figure 1.29 Panel A). The engine of this growth has been the Chinese corporate bond market. China has gone from representing a negligible part of the region's total issuance to more than two-thirds in 2021. While issuances by Japanese companies almost doubled from 2000 to 2021 in absolute terms, the relative share of Japanese issuances decreased significantly, from 56% in 2000 to 13% in 2021 (Figure 1.29 Panel B).

The total amount of outstanding non-financial corporate bonds issued by Asian companies reached USD 3.8 trillion in 2021 (Figure 1.29 Panel C). This represents 25% of global outstanding amounts, and issuance represents 39% of the global total (Figure 1.29 Panel D). China alone accounts for 27% of global issuance and 15% of global outstanding amounts.

Figure 1.29. Asian non-financial corporate bonds landscape

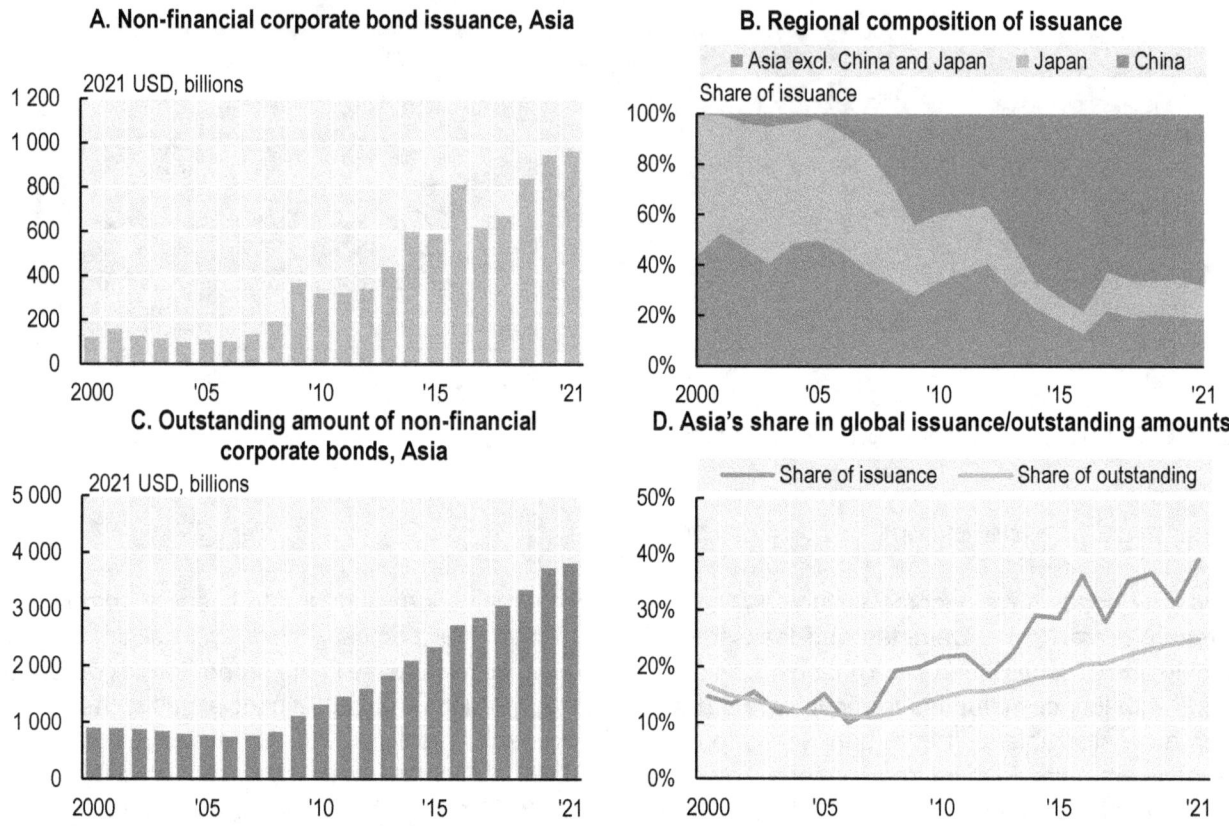

Source: OECD Capital Market Series dataset, Thomson Reuters Eikon, see Annex for details.

As bond markets have grown, the average credit quality of corporate bonds has decreased from the high levels of the early 2000s. The value-weighted average rating of Asian issues has decreased from above A (16.4 on a numerically codified scale where 21 represents the highest rating, AAA) in 2000 to slightly below BBB+ (13.8) in 2021, i.e. about two notches above the lowest investment grade rating (Figure 1.30 Panel A). This is somewhat higher than the average rating globally, towards which Asian issuers have converged since about 2015 after historically having had a higher average rating. However, this development has not been driven by a marked increase in non-investment grade issuance. The non-investment grade (or "high-yield") bond market has remained at very low levels throughout the analysed period, representing 3.7% of total issuance in the region in 2020, although growing to 6.0% in 2021. This is compared to a significantly higher share of 22.5% globally (Figure 1.30 Panel B). The Japanese non-investment grade market is small (although the share of non-investment grade issuance has varied sharply between years over the period analysed). The non-investment grade share of issuance in China was 4.5% in 2020 and 3.1% in 2021. It follows that the reduction in average ratings observed in Panel A is driven primarily by a change in composition within the investment grade category from higher ratings towards lower investment grade ratings. In addition, the change in regional composition of issuance shown in Panel B of Figure 1.29 also affects the Asian rating index.

Figure 1.30. Credit quality of non-financial corporate bonds

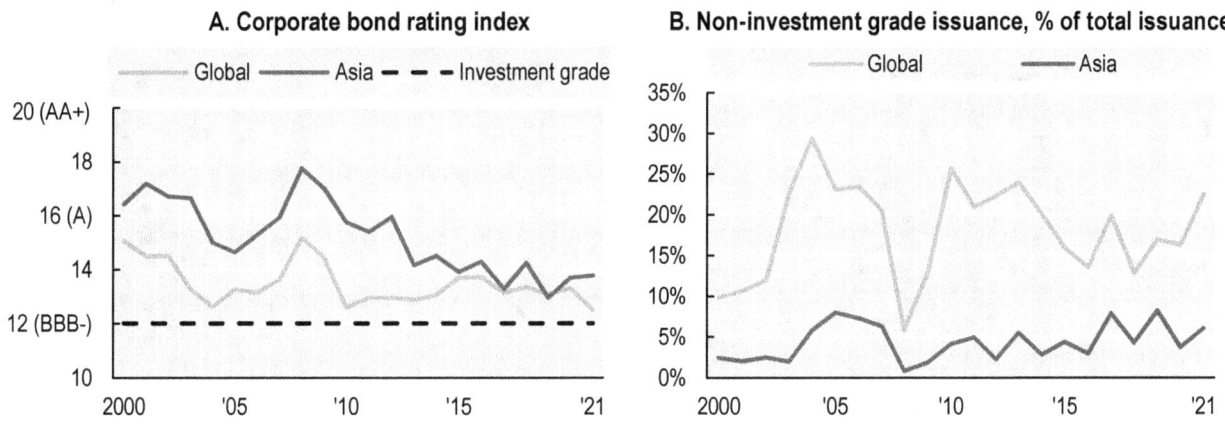

Source: OECD Capital Market Series dataset, Thomson Reuters Eikon, see Annex for details.

Indeed, the composition of investment grade issuance has moved towards lower ratings in recent years, globally as well as in Asia. As shown in Figure 1.31, at the end of 2020, bonds in the BBB category – the lowest investment grade category – represented the largest share of investment grade issuance in both Asia (50.2%) and globally (51.3%). The increase (and corresponding decrease in the A grade categories) has been particularly pronounced in Asia, where the share of BBB rated bonds increased from 5.9% in 2009 to more than half in 2020. However, in 2021 the share in Asia dropped to 36.8%, making A grades the largest category at 45.8%. Meanwhile, the share of BBB rated bonds in investment grade issuance globally grew to 57.5%.

Figure 1.31. Composition of investment grade issuance

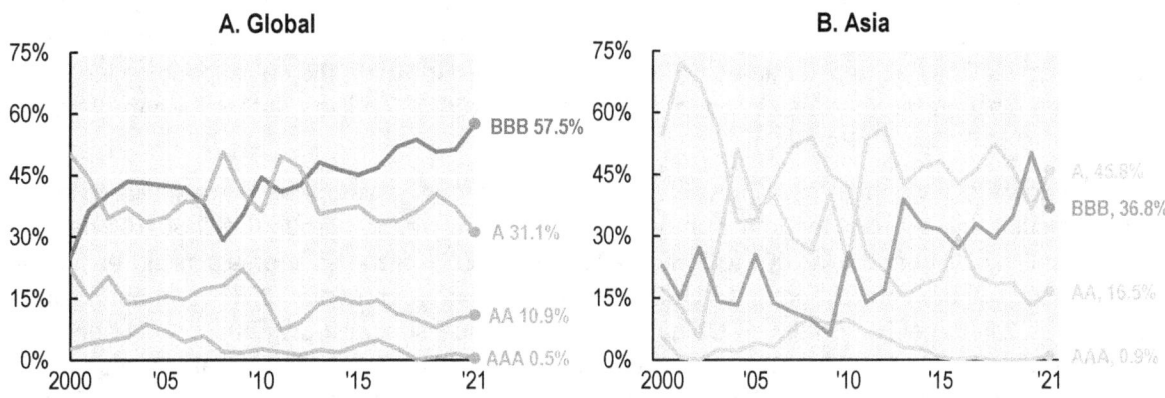

Source: OECD Capital Market Series dataset, Thomson Reuters Eikon, see Annex for details.

As Asian bond markets have grown, the industry composition of issuance has also changed (Figure 1.32). Most notably, industrial companies' issuance has more than doubled, increasing from 23% in 2008 to 52% in 2021. The largest corresponding decreases have taken place in the utilities (from 27% in 2008 to 13% in 2021) and telecommunication industries (8% to 4%). The smallest industry in terms of bond issuance in Asia is healthcare, which represented 2% of total issuance at the end of 2020 (although increasing from 1% in 2008). In 2021 the share fell again, to below 1%.

Figure 1.32. Industry distribution of non-financial corporate bonds issued in Asia

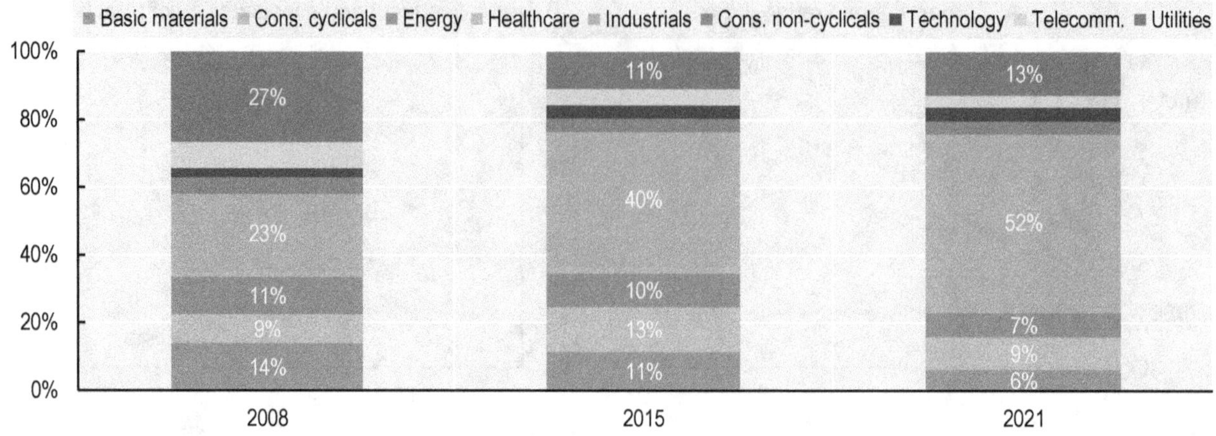

Source: OECD Capital Market Series dataset, Thomson Reuters Eikon, see Annex for details.

Figure 1.33 shows the distribution of the number of corporate bonds issued across five different size categories over the past two decades, along with the median issue size. Globally, up until 2012 the trend was an increase in the median issue size and a shrinking share of the number of bond issuances taking place in the two smallest categories (below USD 100 million), which are the most attainable for smaller growth companies looking to access bond markets. However, since 2012 the median issue size globally has decreased from USD 307 million to USD 128 million in 2021. Simultaneously, the share of bonds below USD 100 million (i.e. the two smallest brackets) more than doubled from 18% to 43% of the total number of bonds issued (Panel A). Broadly, the trend has been similar in advanced Asia. During the same period, median issue size decreased from USD 203 million in 2012 to USD 51 million in 2021, while the two smallest size categories increased significantly, from 15% of the total number of issues to 71% (Panel B). However, the opposite is true for emerging and developing Asia (excluding China). The median issue size has remained roughly similar (USD 71 million to USD 69 million), and the share of the two smallest categories has decreased modestly, from 59% to 57%. However, the corresponding increase has primarily taken place in the fourth size group, between USD 250-500 million, rather than the largest size bracket (>=USD 500 million) (Panel C).

Panels D-F show the developments in individual countries. In Japan, developments are similar to the global trend. In particular, the share of the total number of issues by the second group (USD 50-100 million) has increased significantly, from 5% in 2008 to 38% in 2021 (Panel D). Korea has seen a similar trend, although with concentration in the smallest group (< USD 50 million), which represented 66% of the total number of issuances in 2021 (Panel E). Finally, in China the median issue size and distribution between brackets have been relatively stable since 2013. Prior to that, the market was dominated by larger issuances, with the median issue size reaching USD 557 million in 2012 and issues larger than USD 500 million representing 54% of the total number of issues. In 2021, the median issue size was USD 150 million, similar to the global median, and the number of issuances within the smallest two size groups represented 39% of the total, also close to the global figure (Panel F).

Figure 1.33. Median issue size and distribution by size category

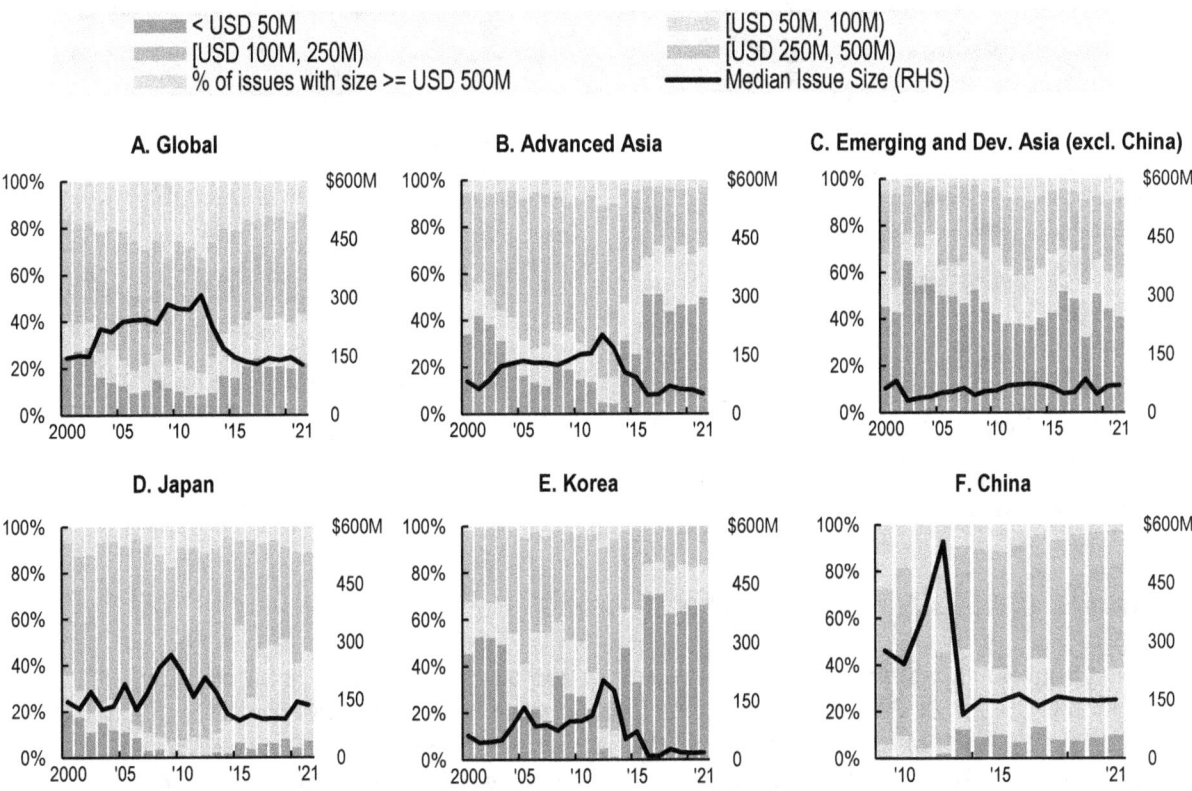

Note: Panel F starts from 2009 since bond issuance by Chinese companies was limited prior to that year.
Source: OECD Capital Market Series dataset, Thomson Reuters Eikon, see Annex for details.

The lion's share of corporate bonds in Asia are listed either on a local exchange (i.e. in the same jurisdiction as where the company is domiciled), issued over the counter (OTC) or not listed. In advanced Asia, and emerging and developing Asia these three categories together make up 91% and 89%, respectively, of the total amount issued over the past two decades. In advanced Asia, OTC trading is the most common category, representing 61% of total issuance. Japan, in particular, has a significant share of OTC trading, which accounted for 85% of total issuance from 2000 to 2021. The corresponding figure in emerging and developing Asia is lower at 20%. Instead, listing on local exchanges is more common within this category, representing 44% of total issuance compared to 16% in advanced Asia (Figure 1.34 Panel A).

With respect to currency composition, the Japanese Yen and Korean Won dominate issues in advanced Asia, representing 49% and 26% of total issuance, respectively. Unsurprisingly, issuance in emerging and developing Asia is done primarily in Chinese Yuan, which accounts for 82% of total issuance. The US dollar (USD) is an important foreign currency in all regions, representing 13% of all issuance in advanced Asia and 9% in emerging and developing Asia. Looking at the individual jurisdictions, the US dollar is most widely used in Korea, where it accounts for 12% of issuance, followed by China and Japan with 7% and 6%, respectively (Figure 1.34 Panel B). In addition to the US dollar, other important currencies in advanced Asia are the domestic currencies from Chinese Taipei and Singapore, and the Euro. In emerging and developing Asia, the Thai Baht and Indian Rupee make up the largest part of the "other" category in Panel B.

Figure 1.34. Distribution of corporate bond issuances by exchange and currency, 2000-21

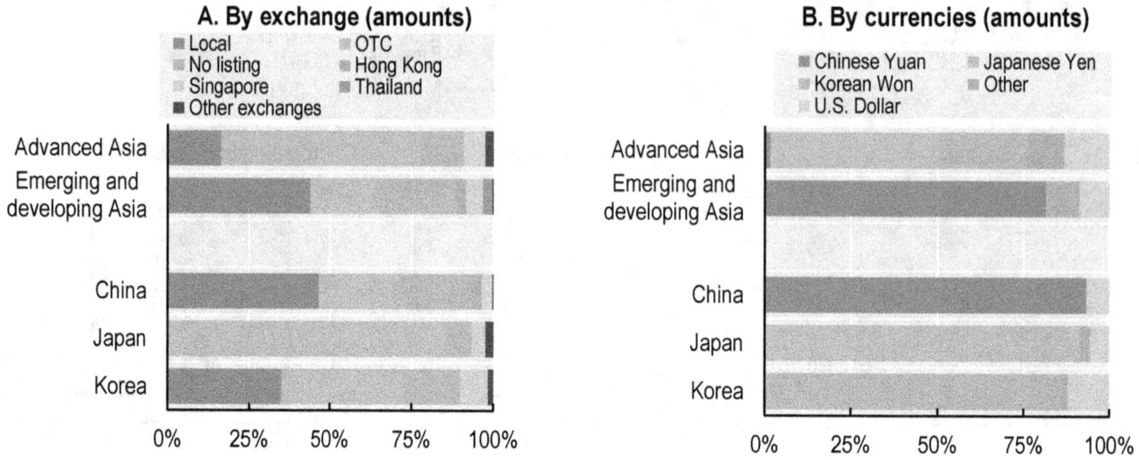

Note: In Panel A, any OTC issuance is classified as OTC, even if the issue is registered as local OTC.
Source: OECD Capital Market Series dataset, Thomson Reuters Eikon, see Annex for details.

1.4. Trends in ASEAN capital markets

Companies from Southeast Asia raised a total of USD 265 billion and USD 528 billion between 1990 and 2021 through IPOs and SPOs, respectively. During the entire period, proceeds of ASEAN IPOs and SPOs accounted for 11% each of Asian IPOs and SPOs. The share of ASEAN IPOs and SPOs was 18.3% and 28.8% in total Asian IPOs over the 1990-99 period, which decreased to 8.7% and 9.9% during the 2009-21 period (Figure 1.35 Panels A and C). Non-financial companies made up 86% and 71% of the total IPO and SPO proceeds over the entire period from 1990 to 2021, respectively. For both, the industrials sector represents a significant part (Figure 1.35 Panels B and D).

Companies from ASEAN countries raised a total of USD 1.5 trillion through corporate bonds over the period from 1990 to 2021. The share of companies from financial industry was significantly higher than for IPOs and SPOs, at 55% of total corporate bond proceeds over the same period. Over the entire period from 1990 to 2021, ASEAN corporate bonds accounted for 6.9% of total Asian corporate bond proceeds. The share of ASEAN corporate bonds was 9.5% of total corporate bond proceeds of Asia over the 1990-99 period (Figure 1.36 Panel A), however, the share decreased to 6.1% during the 2009-21 period. Companies in the industrials, energy and utilities sectors made up a significant part of corporate bonds over the entire period (Figure 1.36 Panel B).

Figure 1.35. Initial and secondary public offerings by ASEAN companies

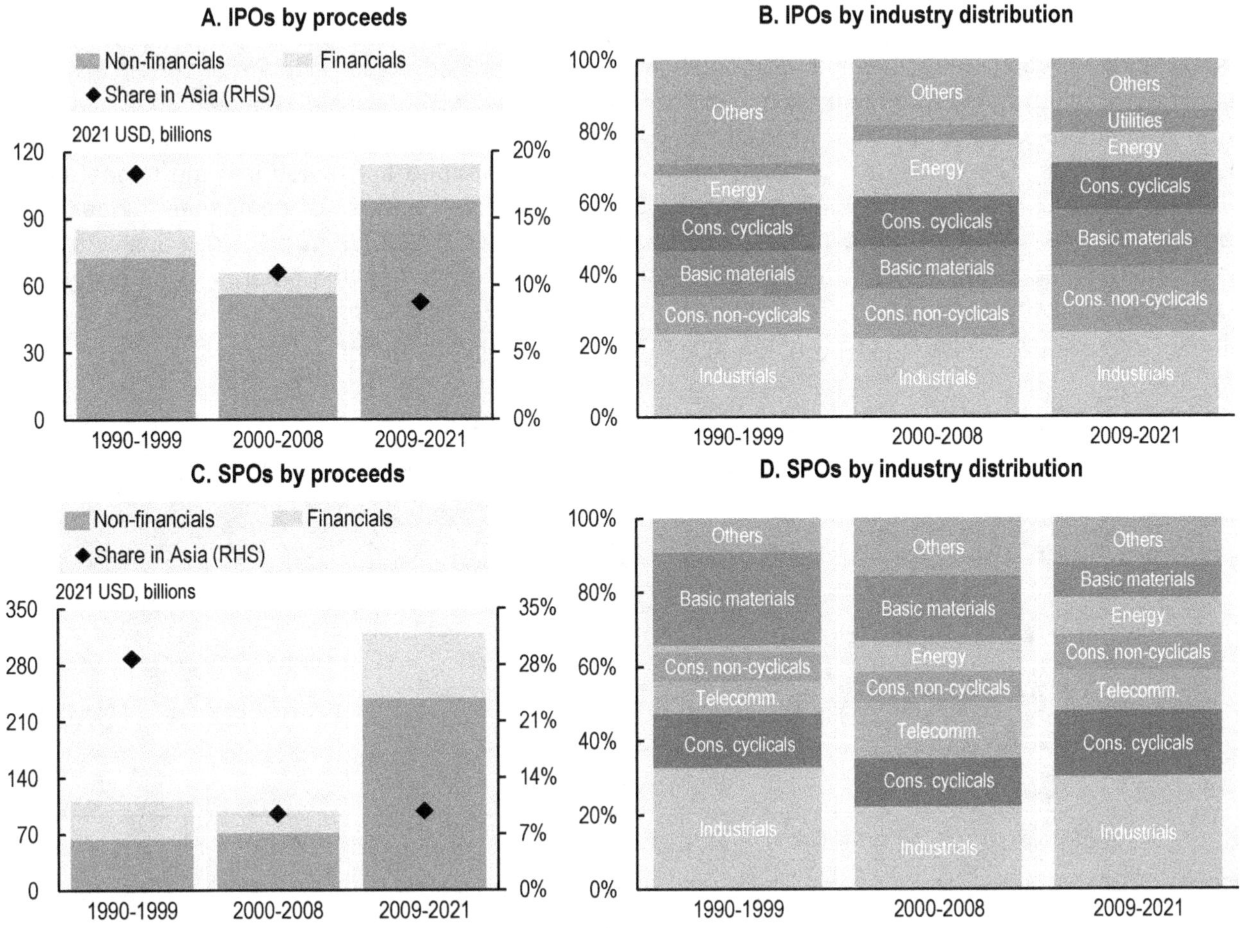

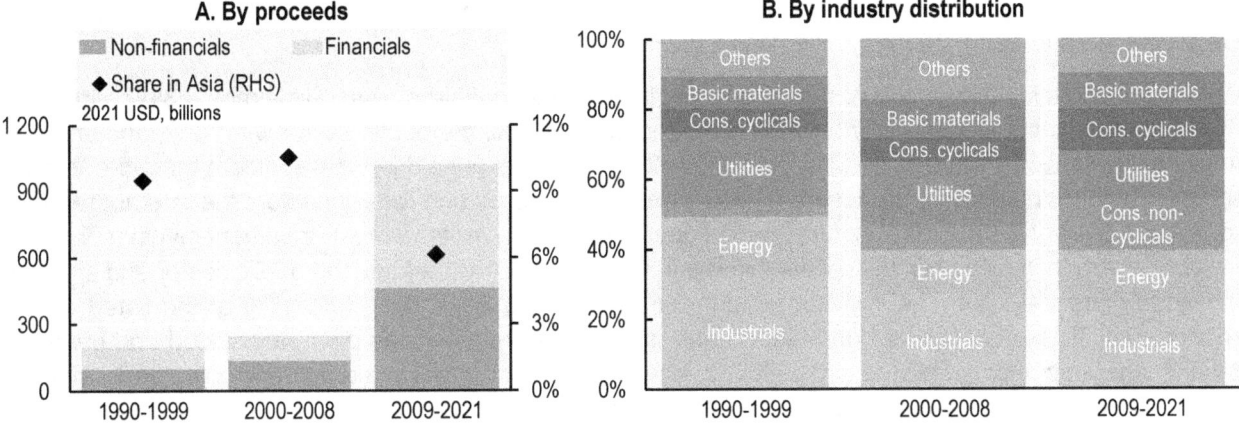

Source: OECD Capital Market Series dataset, see Annex for details.

Figure 1.36. Corporate bond issuances by ASEAN companies

Source: OECD Capital Market Series dataset, Thomson Reuters Eikon, see Annex for details.

1.5. Ownership structure of listed companies

Asian companies significantly influence today's corporate ownership landscape. The increasing participation of Asian companies in public equity markets has shifted the importance of certain investors and affected the ownership concentration at the company level on a global scale. Between 2009 and 2020, 47% of all public equity in the world was raised by Asian companies. This is a marked increase from 22% during the 1990s. The dynamism of Asian equity markets has turned the region into the largest equity market by number of listed companies, hosting 54% of the total number of companies globally and representing one-third of the global market capitalisation by the end of 2020 (Figure 1.37). Advanced Asian equity markets account for 30% of the global number of listed companies and emerging and developing Asian equity markets account for 24%. ASEAN markets, despite not representing a large share of the global market capitalisation, host 8% of the total number of listed companies globally.

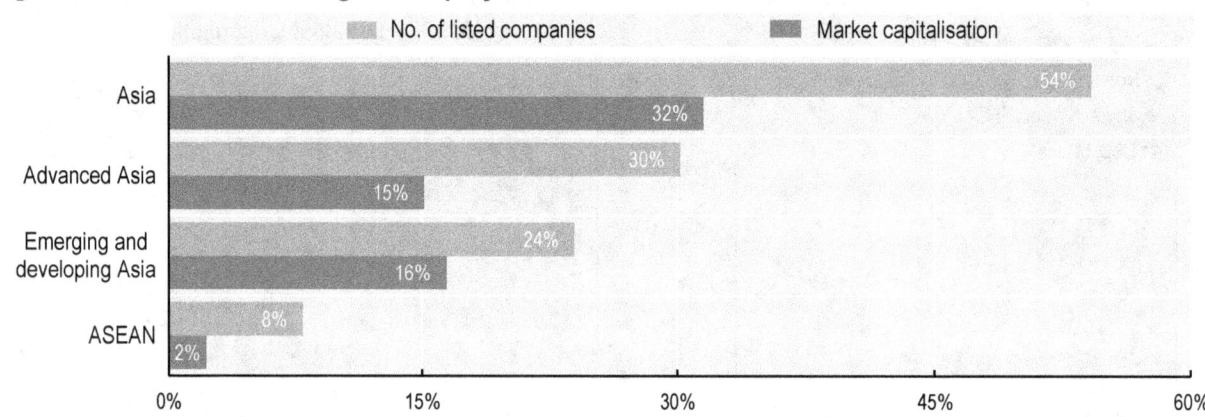

Figure 1.37. Asia's share in global equity markets as of end-2020

Source: OECD Capital Market Series dataset, FactSet, Thomson Reuters, Bloomberg, see Annex for details.

At the end of 2020, there were 40 531 listed companies in the world with a combined market value of USD 105 trillion. This section uses ownership information from almost 26 000 listed companies from 92 different markets. Together, these companies make up 98% of total global stock market value. Using the records of owners for each company, the investors were classified into five categories: private corporations, public sector, strategic individuals, institutional investors and other free float (De La Cruz, Medina and Tang, 2019[14]) (see Annex for details).

At the global level, the largest investor category is institutional investors, who own almost 43% of the world market capitalisation, followed by private corporations with 11%, the public sector with 10%, and strategic individuals with 9% (Figure 1.38). The remaining 27% free-float is held by shareholders that do not reach the threshold for mandatory disclosure of their ownership records and retail investors that are not required to do so. Contrary to the global picture, institutional investors are not the most prominent investor category in Asia, where they own only 18% of the listed equity. Instead, corporations, the public sector and strategic individuals are key investors in Asian equity markets owning 20%, 17% and 14% of the listed equity, respectively. The presence of corporations and institutional investors as owners of listed companies is much higher in companies listed in developed Asia compared to those listed on developing and emerging Asian markets. Conversely, emerging and developing Asia shows a higher ownership of the public sector and strategic individuals in listed companies. Notably, companies listed on ASEAN stock exchanges have the highest share of corporations as owners at 32%.

Figure 1.38. Investors' holdings as of end-2020

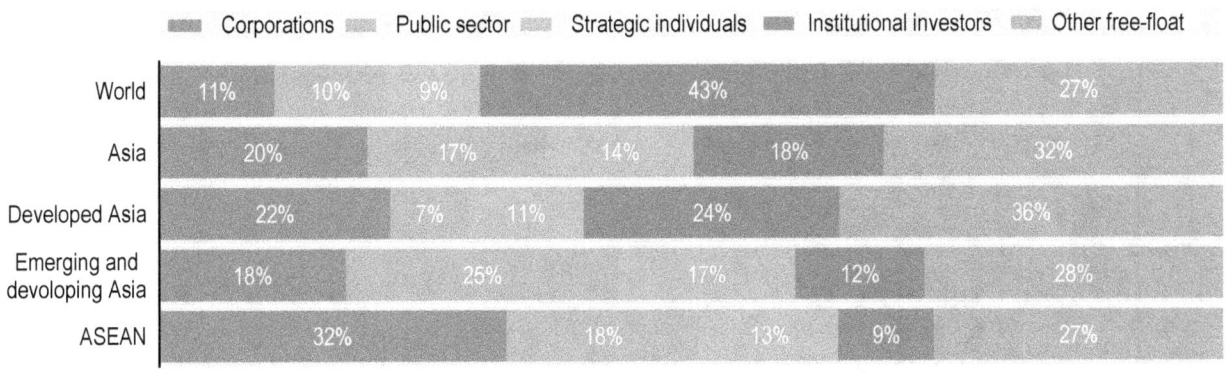

Source: OECD Capital Market Series dataset, FactSet, Thomson Reuters, Bloomberg, see Annex for details.

There are significant differences between jurisdictions with respect to the relative importance of each category of investors (Figure 1.39). Corporations are important investors in Sri Lanka, the Philippines, Pakistan, Indonesia and India, where they own over one-third of the listed equity. The public sector is an important owner in Malaysia, China and Viet Nam, owning over 25% of the listed equity. Strategic individuals hold a significant share of the listed equity in Hong Kong (China), Thailand, China, Bangladesh and the Philippines. Institutional investors are important owners of listed equity in Japan, Chinese Taipei and India where they hold over 20% of the listed equity. In Hong Kong (China) and Korea their equity holdings account for 18% of the market capitalisation. The presence of institutional investors remains modest in mainland China, but with the progressive inclusion of A-shares in investable indices it is expected to grow.

Figure 1.39. Investors' holdings in Asian markets as of end-2020

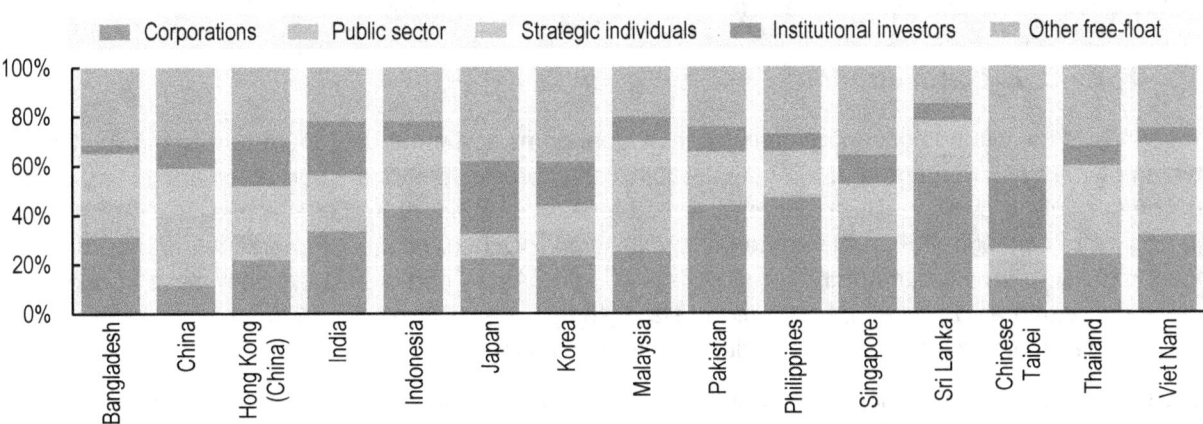

Source: OECD Capital Market Series dataset, FactSet, Thomson Reuters, Bloomberg, see Annex for details.

There are also significant differences across markets with respect to non-domestic ownership (Figure 1.40). For example, in Singapore, Pakistan, Sri Lanka, Chinese Taipei and Indonesia, around 30% of listed equity belongs to non-domestic investors. However, different categories of investors are responsible for non-domestic ownership. In Singapore, Pakistan, Sri Lanka and Indonesia over half of the non-domestic ownership is made up by corporations whereas in Chinese Taipei 85% of it is in the hands of institutional investors. Hong Kong (China) has the highest level of non-domestic investment, with

CORPORATE FINANCE IN ASIA AND THE COVID-19 CRISIS © OECD 2022

mainland Chinese investors holding over 50% of it. In terms of categories, corporations hold 34% and institutional investors 27% of non-domestic holdings in companies listed in Hong Kong (China).

Figure 1.40. Non-domestic ownership in Asian markets by category of investor as of end-2020

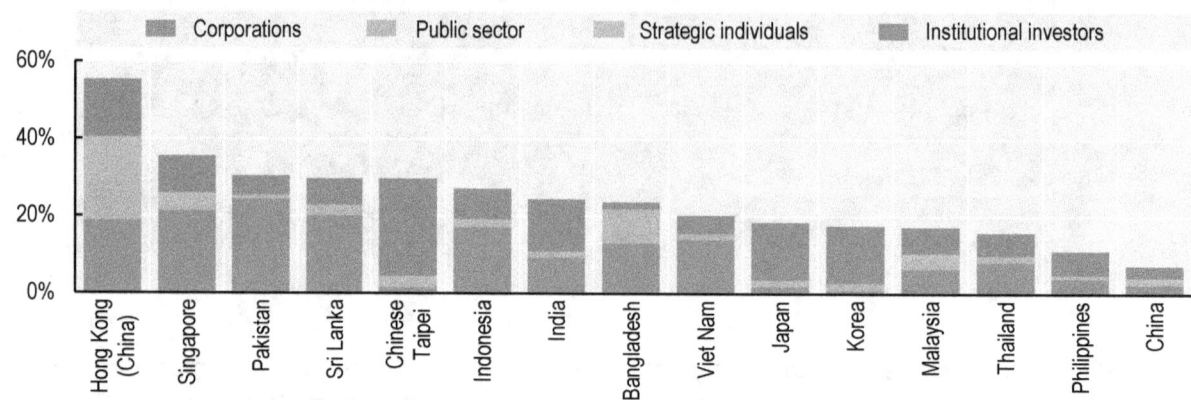

Source: OECD Capital Market Series dataset, FactSet, Thomson Reuters, Bloomberg, see Annex for details.

Non-domestic ownership in many markets is also driven by the presence of global institutional investors. The markets in the region with the highest presence of non-domestic institutional investors are Chinese Taipei, Japan, Hong Kong (China), Korea and India where they hold over 13% of the listed equity. The growing use of indices by institutional investors along with the growing share of corporate equity they own, has led to important differences with respect to institutional ownership between markets and companies that are included in a major index and those that are not. Japan, for example, is the second largest country by weighting in the MSCI World Index (around 7% of the index), after the US market. The markets that are included in large investable indices with higher weights show a significantly higher share of institutional investment, as is the case for Japan, China, Korea, Chinese Taipei and India.

1.5.1. Ownership concentration

The degree of ownership concentration in an individual company is not only important to the relationship between owners and managers. It may also require focus on the relationship between controlling owners and non-controlling owners. The ownership structure in most markets today is characterised by a fairly high degree of concentration at the company level. Asian listed companies, in particular in emerging and developing Asia, have contributed to this increase. Since Asian companies typically have a controlling shareholder, either a corporation, family or the state, shifts towards Asian emerging markets globally have increased the dominance of companies with controlling owners.

Ownership concentration in listed companies is higher in Asia than globally and in advanced markets outside the region. Figure 1.41 shows the share of companies with different levels of ownership for the three largest shareholders at the company level. In 28% of the world's listed companies, the three largest shareholders together hold between 10% and 29% of the equity. In 29% of the listed companies, the three largest shareholders hold between 30-49%, and in 42% of them, the largest three shareholders hold more than 50% of the equity. The three largest shareholders own a total of less than 10% in only 0.6% of the world's listed companies. Importantly, in Asia the three largest shareholders own over 50% of the equity in almost half of the listed companies in the region. Concentration patterns also differ between companies listed in advanced Asian markets and those listed in emerging and developing Asian markets, where the share of companies with the highest level of ownership concentration (i.e. over 50%) is almost 60%. Importantly, ASEAN markets show the highest levels of ownership concentration as the three largest shareholders own over 50% of the equity in almost 70% of listed companies.

Figure 1.41. Ownership concentration by the largest three shareholders as of end-2020

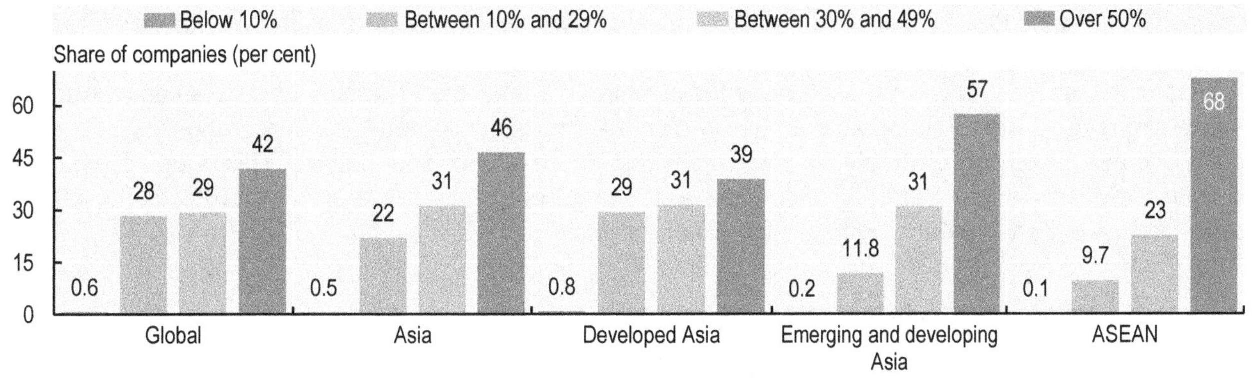

[Legend: Below 10% | Between 10% and 29% | Between 30% and 49% | Over 50%]

Share of companies (per cent)

Region	Below 10%	Between 10% and 29%	Between 30% and 49%	Over 50%
Global	0.6	28	29	42
Asia	0.5	22	31	46
Developed Asia	0.8	29	31	39
Emerging and developing Asia	0.2	11.8	31	57
ASEAN	0.1	9.7	23	68

Note: The figure shows the number of companies with different levels of ownership by the three largest shareholders as a share of the total number of listed companies in each region.
Source: OECD Capital Market Series dataset, FactSet, Thomson Reuters, Bloomberg, see Annex for details.

The regional picture masks some important differences at the economy level. Figure 1.42 shows the ownership concentration at the company level for each market. It shows the average combined holdings of the largest single, largest 3 and largest 20 owners. For example, in Indonesia the average combined holdings of a company's three largest owners add up to over 55% of the equity capital. Ownership in listed companies is also concentrated in Singapore, Hong Kong (China), the Philippines and Sri Lanka where the largest three shareholders on average own over 45% of the equity in each listed company. Other economies in the region show a significantly lower level of concentration, notably Korea, Japan and Chinese Taipei. In general, the level of concentration of ownership in the region is similar to levels in Latin America and in some other emerging markets.

Figure 1.42. Ownership concentration at the company level as of end-2020

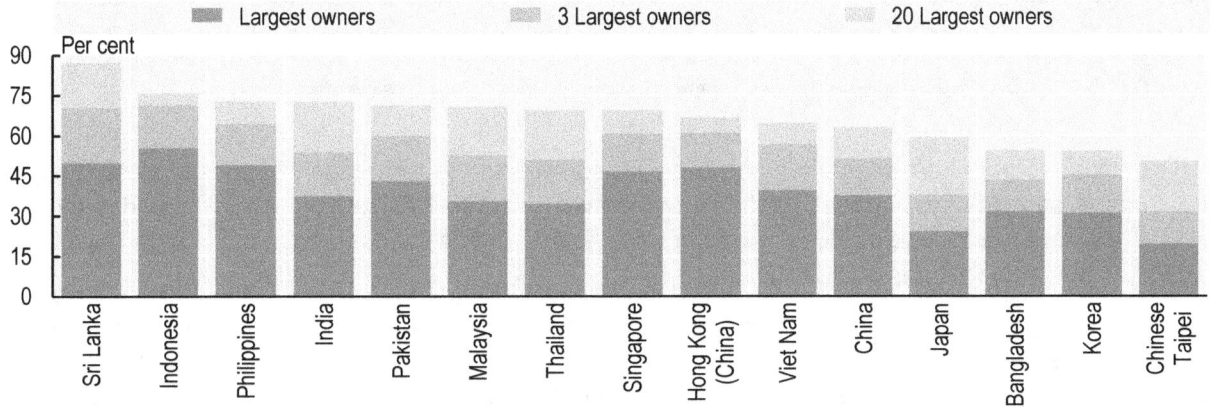

Source: OECD Capital Market Series dataset, FactSet, Thomson Reuters, Bloomberg, see Annex for details.

1.5.2. Corporations as owners

As previously shown in Figure 1.38, corporations are significant owners of equity in the region. Indeed, they hold 20% of the regional market capitalisation and in eight out of the 15 jurisdictions for which ownership information is available, corporations hold over 30% of the listed equity. In several of these jurisdictions non-domestic entities are responsible for corporate ownership (Table 1.2). For example, in

Sri Lanka, Pakistan and Singapore, over 20% of the market capitalisation is owned by non-domestic corporations. In Asia in general, it is also common that listed corporations are owned by other listed companies. The second to last column in the table below shows the share of the market capitalisation owned by another public corporation. Jurisdictions with high overall corporate ownership have high ownership by other listed companies. This is the case in Sri Lanka, the Philippines, Pakistan and Indonesia where almost a quarter of the listed equity in each market is held by other listed corporations. However, in many of these cases, this ownership is made up by non-domestic listed companies. This is the case notably in Singapore, Sri Lanka, Pakistan, Indonesia and Hong Kong (China), where over 10% of the market capitalisation is owned by non-domestic listed corporations.

Table 1.2. Corporations as owners by location and listed status as of end-2020

	Share of market capitalisation owned by:				
	Corporations	Non-domestic corporations	Domestic corporations	Publicly listed corporations	Non-domestic public listed corporations
Sri Lanka	57%	20%	37%	43%	18%
Philippines	47%	4%	43%	30%	3%
Pakistan	44%	24%	19%	25%	17%
Indonesia	43%	17%	25%	24%	16%
India	33%	9%	24%	16%	7%
Viet Nam	31%	14%	17%	18%	9%
Bangladesh	31%	13%	18%	11%	9%
Singapore	30%	21%	9%	24%	19%
Malaysia	25%	6%	19%	10%	5%
Thailand	24%	8%	16%	17%	7%
Korea	23%	1%	22%	21%	1%
Japan	22%	2%	20%	18%	1%
Hong Kong (China)	22%	19%	3%	16%	14%
Chinese Taipei	13%	2%	12%	7%	0%
China	12%	2%	9%	4%	2%

Source: OECD Capital Market Series dataset, FactSet, Thomson Reuters, Bloomberg, see Annex for details.

The significant corporate ownership in the region also reflects the existence of intricate company group structures. A sample of the largest 100 listed companies in several Asian jurisdictions provides evidence that these companies have over 60 subsidiaries on average. This is the case in China, Hong Kong (China), Japan, Malaysia and Singapore (OECD, 2022[15]).

Company groups can support economic growth and employment through economies of scale and synergies. If adequately managed, they can foster cross-border investments and operations through multinational companies, and are useful for the safeguarding of intellectual property rights. Reduced need for external finance, lower informational asymmetries, lower transaction costs and less dependence on contract enforcement instruments are other benefits of company groups. Likewise, the incorporation of listed subsidiaries or unlisted joint ventures can stimulate entrepreneurship by better incentivising managers to innovate and have their success recognised by shareholders (OECD, 2020[16]).

However, company groups raise important challenges with respect to corporate governance, including how to protect minority shareholders' interests against controlling shareholders and how to effectively oversee various risks arising from group structures. OECD (2022[15]) provides a set of good practices for corporate governance of company groups in Asia. These recommendations focus on issues related to risk management, governance policies, access to key information about activities of group companies, independent directors, permissible group structures, disclosure and controlling persons.

1.5.3. The public sector as an owner

The importance of listed companies under public sector ownership has increased worldwide during the past two decades, mostly reflecting the listing of minority stakes of state-owned enterprises (SOEs) as a first step toward or as an alternative to complete privatisation. The partial privatisation of many state-owned companies through stock market listings in Asia has contributed to making Asian stock markets more dynamic and attractive. It is notable that in Asia, and in many Asian emerging markets in particular, privatisation through stock market listings has not led to any change in control. Today states have controlling stakes in a large number of listed companies. Globally, the public sector held USD 10.7 trillion of listed equity as of end-2020, which was almost 10% of global market capitalisation. In Asia this share is 17% of the regional market capitalisation.

Table 1.3 shows the public sector ownership by four different investor types. The first type of public sector investor includes both central and regional governments that hold stakes in publicly listed companies. The second type corresponds to public pension funds, which manage mandatory pension schemes or/and retirement savings of public sector employees. The third type is sovereign wealth funds (SWFs) that serve as central state ownership agencies with controlling or non-controlling stakes in publicly listed companies. They include savings funds, stabilisation funds and pension reserve funds. The fourth type is financial and non-financial SOEs that hold shares in listed corporations. In emerging and developing Asia, central and local governments are the largest public sector investor type, accounting for 73% of all public sector holdings in listed equity, followed by SOEs and SWFs. This picture is different in advanced Asia where SWFs is the largest public sector owner (33%), ahead of public pension funds (31%).

Table 1.3. Public sector holdings as of end-2020

	Public sector holdings (USD million)	As share of public sector holdings			
		Governments	Public pension funds	Sovereign wealth funds	State-owned enterprises
Advanced Asia	660 280	24%	31%	33%	12%
Emerging and developing Asia	4 607 152	73%	2%	13%	12%
Bangladesh	2 525	75%	0%	0%	25%
China	3 984 075	76%	1%	14%	9%
Hong Kong (China)	30 692	99%	0%	0%	1%
India	275 936	52%	0%	0%	48%
Indonesia	75 727	92%	1%	0%	7%
Japan	134 774	56%	4%	0%	40%
Korea	252 993	8%	77%	13%	3%
Malaysia	140 155	18%	41%	12%	29%
Pakistan	5 247	75%	1%	0%	24%
Philippines	1 852	7%	90%	0%	3%
Singapore	170 216	0%	0%	87%	12%
Sri Lanka	733	29%	49%	0%	22%
Chinese Taipei	71 604	48%	4%	48%	0%
Thailand	79 917	61%	8%	0%	31%
Viet Nam	40 985	80%	0%	10%	10%

Source: OECD Capital Market Series dataset, FactSet, Thomson Reuters, Bloomberg, see Annex for details.

Table 1.4 provides an overview of the magnitude of listed companies controlled by the public sector. Any company in which at least one ultimate parent is a government which owns 25% of the shares is classified as controlled by the state.[3] By the end of 2020, 1 677 listed companies globally had the state as a controlling shareholder. Of this number, 1 315 companies were listed on Asian stock exchanges with a total market capitalisation of USD 7.4 trillion. These listed firms under state control are often among the largest listed firms in their jurisdictions, for example representing about 44% of the listed equity in China, 43% in Malaysia and 39% in Viet Nam. The average public sector ownership in these companies in each market is shown in Table 1.4 and corresponds to the ownership of all public sector investors and not necessary to only one government. Notably, the controlled firms have an average public sector ownership over 50% of the listed equity.

Table 1.4. Listed companies in Asia under state control as of end-2020

	Market cap. of state controlled companies (USD million)	No. of listed companies under state control	Average state holdings[4]	State-controlled listed companies (share of total market capitalisation)	State-controlled listed companies (share of total number of companies)
China	5 434 950	773	50%	44%	26%
Malaysia	180 573	59	57%	43%	12%
Viet Nam	62 040	37	52%	39%	21%
Indonesia	125 977	46	65%	26%	9%
Singapore	113 108	17	47%	26%	6%
Thailand	121 267	18	51%	24%	5%
Bangladesh	8 483	11	64%	23%	11%
Pakistan	7 539	12	67%	17%	9%
Hong Kong (China)	686 252	194	53%	15%	12%
India	285 769	101	68%	11%	9%
Sri Lanka	664	5	49%	5%	8%
Chinese Taipei	63 864	9	37%	4%	3%
Japan	245 175	16	46%	4%	0%
Korea	54 178	16	54%	3%	1%
Philippines	306	1	38%	0%	1%

Source: OECD Capital Market Series dataset, FactSet, Thomson Reuters, Bloomberg, see Annex for details.

2 Navigating the pandemic

This chapter provides information on how Asian corporations were able to access financing via public equity and corporate bond markets during the COVID-19 pandemic. It tracks financing activity on a monthly basis and provides a detailed characterisation of the use of market-based financing at the industry and market level. It also takes stock of the fiscal and regulatory measures taken by Asian authorities in response to the pandemic to mitigate the effects on the corporate sector.

2.1. Market-based financing during the pandemic

In the wake of the 2008 financial crisis, access to market-based financing gave many corporations the financial resilience that enabled them to overcome a temporary downturn while meeting their obligations to employees, creditors and suppliers. In 2020 and 2021, during the COVID-19 pandemic, corporations' access to capital markets was equally important to mitigate liquidity shortages and avoid defaults and bankruptcies. From a longer-term perspective, structural policies that facilitate efficient and affordable market-based financing of viable companies will be crucial in order to strengthen long-term resilience and help companies endure future shocks.

When discussing the long-term implications of the crisis, it is important to understand how capital markets reacted to the COVID-19 crisis. This section provides key indicators on how the non-financial corporate sector used public equity and corporate bond markets throughout 2020 and 2021, analysing the short-term impact of the COVID-19 crisis on market-based financing.

2.1.1. Public equity markets

In 2020 and 2021, the non-financial corporate sector made extensive use of public equity markets. The total amount of capital raised by non-financial companies through initial public offerings (IPOs) and secondary public offerings (SPOs) reached record values of USD 826 billion in 2020 and USD 1 trillion in 2021. Notably, 44% of the total amount raised globally in both years was raised by Asian non-financial companies, totalling USD 351 billion and USD 454 billion, respectively. At the beginning of 2020, the COVID-19 outbreak caused major uncertainties that translated into high market volatility and a significant decrease in the non-financial corporate sector's use of primary public equity markets. Globally, the total amount of capital raised by non-financial companies during the first quarter of 2020 was considerably lower than the previous five-year average (Figure 2.1). This downturn reversed during the second quarter. Importantly, the third and fourth quarters of 2020 showed a significant increase in the amount of capital raised (driven mostly by SPOs) compared to the previous five-year average.

In Asia, the amount of capital raised during the first quarter of 2020 contracted by around 20% compared to the previous five-year average (Figure 2.1). The decline was most pronounced in advanced Asian markets with a 60% decrease compared to the previous five-year average, while in emerging and developing Asia (excluding China) it declined by around 20%. Japanese and Chinese non-financial corporations' capital raising activity declined by around 35% and 13%, respectively, compared to their historical averages. During the third quarter of 2020, this trend reversed (following the global trend) in Asia, as non-financial companies raised funds amounting to USD 136 billion, with China and Japan accounting for 68% and 19% respectively of that amount.

In the first and second quarters of 2021, the global amount of equity raised via IPOs and SPOs peaked, totalling almost USD 280 billion, twice the average proceeds raised in the 2015-19 period. Primary equity market activity remained vibrant in the second half of 2021, surpassing its historical averages, albeit somewhat lower than in 2020. Similarly, the equity capital raised by Asian companies reached record levels averaging USD 113 billion per quarter. Notably, Chinese companies accounted for 64% of the proceeds raised in public equity markets by Asian companies in 2021, while companies from other emerging and developing Asia represented only 12% and companies from advanced Asia the remaining 24%.

Figure 2.1. Equity capital raised by non-financial companies in public markets in 2020 and 2021

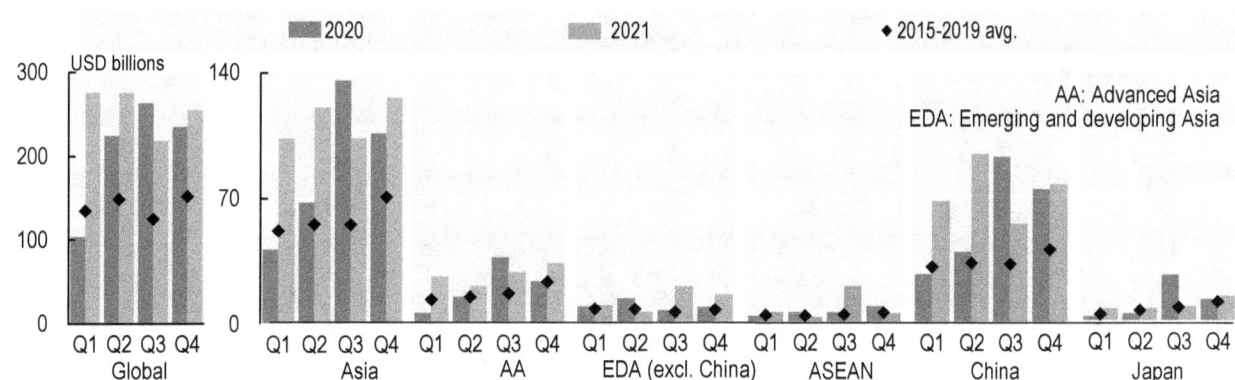

Source: OECD Capital Market Series dataset, see Annex for details.

At the industry level, the total capital raised during the first quarter of 2020 declined in most industries, except for healthcare, consumer non-cyclicals and telecommunications services, both globally and in Asia. Globally, the largest contraction in fundraising through public equity markets took place in the utilities, energy and consumer cyclicals industries (OECD, 2021[2]). In Asia, the contraction of those three industries was more significant than globally. In addition, in Asia the capital raised by basic materials companies decreased significantly (Figure 2.2). In contrast, in the second quarter of 2020, all industries, except for energy and basic materials, raised significantly more capital than the previous five-year average globally (OECD, 2021[2]). In Asia, the energy and telecommunications services industries raised a record amount of funds, six and three times their previous five-year average, respectively, while the basic materials, consumer cyclicals, and technology industries continued their contraction. Notably, the healthcare industry raised USD 50 billion globally during the second quarter, compared to an average of USD 21 billion during the 2015-19 period (OECD, 2021[2]). During the last three-quarters of 2020, Asian companies from the healthcare industry tripled their use of public equity markets compared to the previous five-year average. In the third quarter, every industry, except energy, raised more capital than in the previous five years both globally and in Asia. In the fourth quarter, globally, six out of nine industries raised more capital and, in Asia, seven out of nine industries did.

In 2021, during the first quarter, all industries, with the exception of telecommunications services, raised more capital than in the first quarter of 2020. During the first quarter of 2021, technology companies raised USD 27 billion compared to USD 4.4 billion in 2020 and USD 8.5 billion in 2015-19. Remarkably, in January 2021, the Chinese technology company Kuaishou Technology Co Ltd, conducted its IPO in the Hong Kong (China) market, raising USD 6.2 billion, the largest IPO in Asia in 2021 and the second largest globally. During the second quarter of 2021, consumer cyclicals accounted for 21% of the proceeds raised in the region, more than three times during the same period in 2020. Following the same path as during the fourth quarter of 2020, industrials raised a record of USD 36 billion of public equity, twice the 2015-19 average.

Figure 2.2. IPOs by Asian non-financial companies in 2020 and 2021 by industry

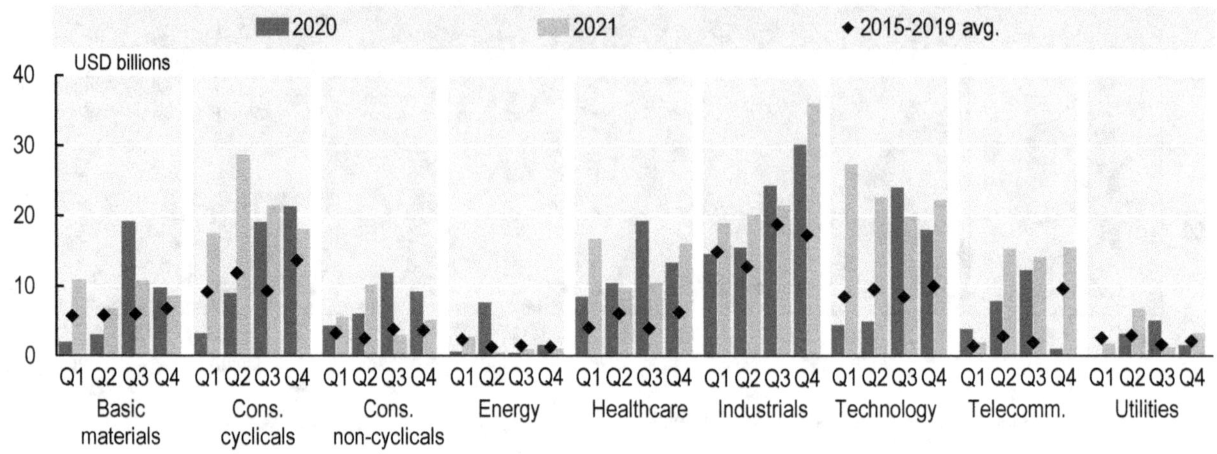

Source: OECD Capital Market Series dataset, see Annex for details.

A closer look at global developments on a monthly basis shows that IPO activity almost came to a halt in March 2020 in several regions, when only six European companies and one US company went public, amounting to a modest total of USD 100 million. In May, the IPO activity in Europe recovered, totalling USD 3.6 billion. In the United States, the rebound was particularly strong in June 2020, when 19 non-financial IPOs raised a record amount of USD 10.6 billion (OECD, 2021[2]). In contrast, 65 Asian non-financial companies went public in March 2020 raising USD 4.6 billion, similar to the previous five-year average. In particular, 29 Chinese non-financial companies raised USD 2.8 billion, accounting for 41% of the global equity raised in March 2020. Also in March, five Indian non-financial companies went public raising USD 1.4 billion, almost four times the previous five-year average. Chinese and Indian non-financial companies accounted for more than 90% of the total IPO funds raised in Asia in March 2020. In February 2020, USD 2.5 billion were raised by ASEAN companies, a significant increase from the USD 105 million raised in the 2015-19 period. The IPO of a Thai consumer non-cyclicals company amounting to USD 2.52 billion made up the lion's share of this amount. IPO activity in advanced Asian markets was modest overall when compared to the previous five-year average; the capital raised was higher than in the previous five years only in February and August (Figure 2.3).

Globally, in the second half of 2020, IPO activity peaked at almost twice the 2015-19 average. This trend was particularly pronounced in China and the United States. In December 2020 alone, companies from China and the United States raised USD 13.4 billion and USD 11.9 billion, respectively, through IPOs (OECD, 2021[2]). Interestingly, in Korea, USD 1.5 billion was raised via IPOs in August and September, four times the amounts raised in the same months of the previous five years. IPO activity in Japan was weak throughout 2020. There was some activity in December when 26 Japanese companies went public, raising a total of USD 1.2 billion, although this was still significantly below the previous five-year average.

In 2021, IPO activity reached a historical record globally. In June and July alone, USD 47 billion and USD 41 billion respectively was raised through IPOs. Throughout the year, the monthly capital raised exceeded historical averages. In Asia, the monthly amount raised via IPOs accounted on average for 42% of the global amounts. IPOs conducted by Chinese companies were substantial during 2021, particularly in January, June and December with more than USD 13 billion in each month. Notably, in March 2021, 80% of the USD 7.4 billion raised by companies from advanced Asia corresponded to IPOs by Korean companies.

Figure 2.3. Monthly initial public offerings by non-financial companies in 2020 and 2021

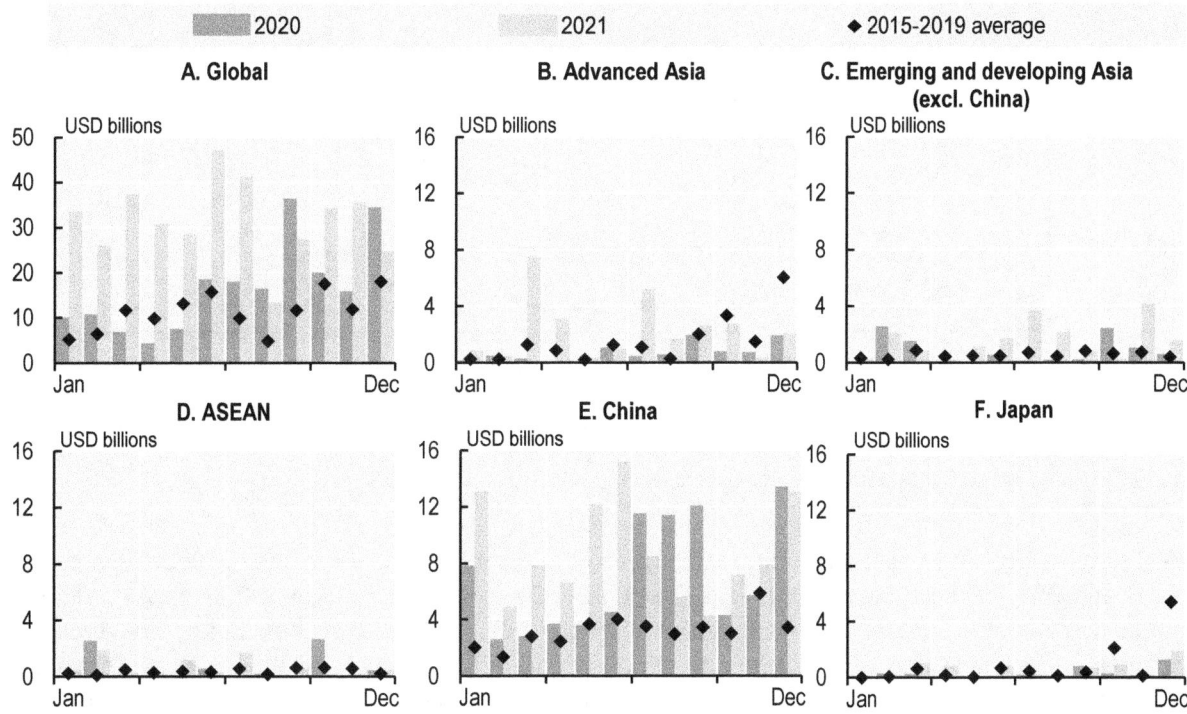

Source: OECD Capital Market Series dataset, see Annex for details.

Overall, in 2020, IPOs were dominated by non-financial companies from emerging and developing Asian markets, mainly driven by Chinese IPOs. As a result, the share of IPOs from advanced Asian markets only accounted for 8% of total Asian IPOs. A comparison against previous five-year averages reveals important differences in how jurisdictions were affected by the COVID-19 crisis (Figure 2.4). Non-financial companies from China and Thailand raised significantly more funds than the previous five-year average, doubling and tripling the amounts, respectively. Indian non-financial companies' use of IPOs was 24% higher. Contrarily, IPOs from Japan and Hong Kong (China) fell by 68% and 87%, respectively. Cambodia, Indonesia, Malaysia, Pakistan and Chinese Taipei, with comparatively smaller public equity markets, also experienced contractions in the amounts of funds raised in 2020, while Bangladesh saw an increase. Non-financial companies from Mongolia, Sri Lanka and Viet Nam did not raise any funds via IPOs in 2020.

In 2021, as global IPO activity reached historical records, more than USD 150 billion were raised via IPOs in Asia. Although Chinese companies accounted for 70% of total Asian proceeds, companies from advanced Asia represented 18%, with companies from emerging and developing Asia (excluding China) making up the remaining 12%. Remarkably, 86 non-financial Korean companies conducted an IPO in 2021, raising a total of almost USD 20 billion, against an average of USD 3.5 billion in 2015-19. Indian companies rank third in terms of proceeds with a total amount of USD 12 billion in 2021 against USD 2.8 billion in 2020. Moreover, although Japanese companies did not exceed their historical IPO amounts, they raised USD 6.9 billion in 2021, ranking fourth in terms of IPOs in Asia. Notably, companies from Indonesia, the Philippines, Singapore and Chinese Taipei raised more proceeds via IPOs in 2021 than in 2020.

Figure 2.4. Initial public offerings by Asian non-financial companies in 2020 and 2021

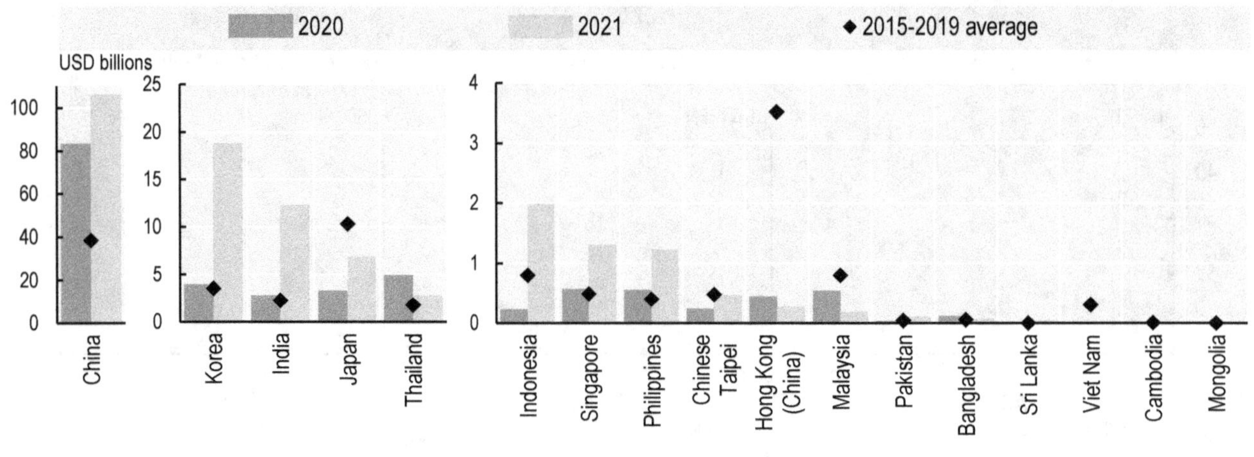

Source: OECD Capital Market Series dataset, see Annex for details.

In 2020, technology and healthcare companies raised the highest amounts of capital globally, accounting for 24% and 23% of the total amount raised through IPOs, respectively (Figure 2.5). In Asia, industrial companies raised the largest share of capital through IPOs, followed by healthcare and technology companies, accounting for 25%, 18% and 17% of the total amount raised in Asia, respectively. US technology companies raised a record amount of USD 24.4 billion, representing more than half of the global proceeds raised by the industry. Chinese technology companies followed with USD 14.6 billion raised, equivalent to 30% of global proceeds. Importantly, US and Chinese healthcare companies raised USD 19.3 billion and USD 15.9 billion, respectively. Industrials companies raised USD 35.5 billion globally in 2020, of which 60% corresponded to Chinese companies. In advanced Asia, IPO proceeds were dominated by consumer cyclicals representing 25% of total proceeds, followed by technology and industrials, representing 23% and 21% respectively. In emerging and developing Asia (excluding China), consumer non-cyclicals accounted for 30% of the proceeds and industrials for 24%. In ASEAN economies, almost 40% of the IPO proceeds were raised by consumer non-cyclicals companies and 19% by basic materials companies.

In 2021, technology companies were even more active than in 2020, raising USD 112 billion globally, representing 30% of global proceeds. Similarly, in China, 28% of the proceeds were raised by technology companies and 18% by healthcare companies. In advanced Asia, technology companies were also significant, accounting for one-third of the proceeds followed by consumer cyclicals which represented 22%. Although consumer non-cyclicals were dominant in ASEAN economies in 2020, in 2021 consumer cyclicals were more important representing 30% of total proceeds.

In India, industrial companies dominated in 2020, with more than half of the capital raised followed by healthcare companies (31%) (Figure 2.6). In 2021, the industry distribution changed considerably, with more than 30% of the proceeds raised by telecommunications, 25% by consumer cyclicals and 19% by basic materials companies. In Korea, the three largest issuers in 2020 were the healthcare (31%), consumer cyclicals (27%) and industrials (24%) industries. In 2021, the picture remained similar with the difference that healthcare companies accounted for 16% and technology companies for 24%. In Japan, technology companies collected 35% of the proceeds raised via IPOs in 2020. This number increased substantially in 2021, when technology companies accounted for more than 60% of the proceeds. In Thailand, consumer non-cyclicals and basic materials companies were the largest issuers in 2020 with 52% and 26% of the funds raised, respectively. In 2021, the energy industry raised the most proceeds, representing almost 70%.

Figure 2.5. IPOs by non-financial companies by industry

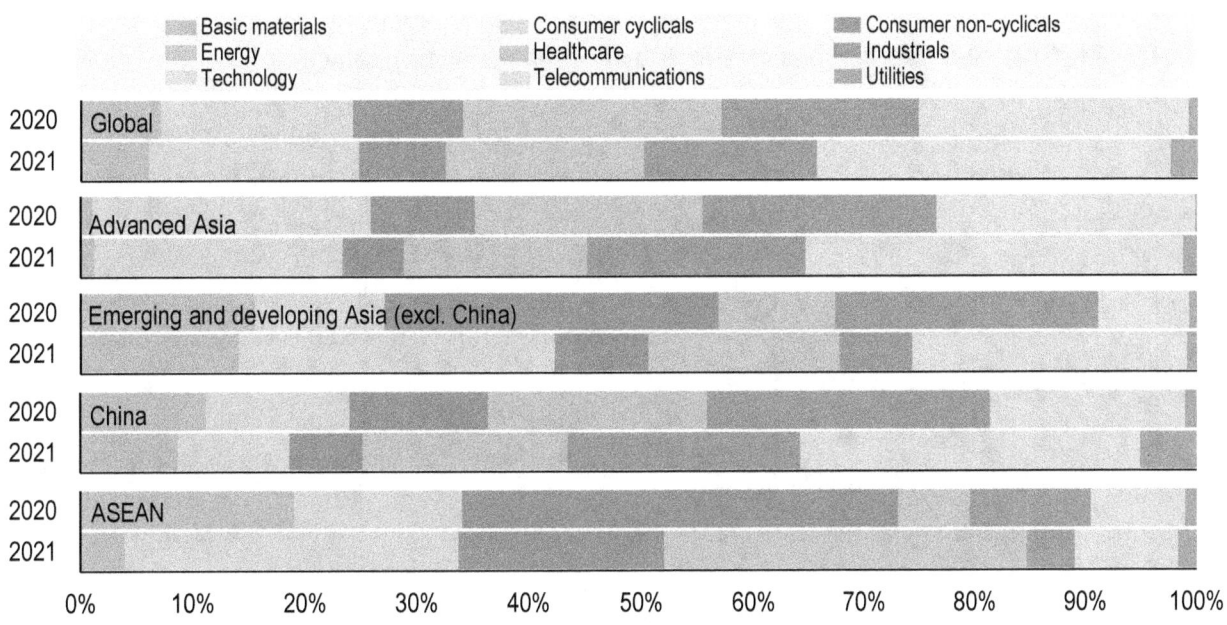

Source: OECD Capital Market Series dataset, see Annex for details.

Figure 2.6 IPOs by non-financial companies by jurisdiction and industry

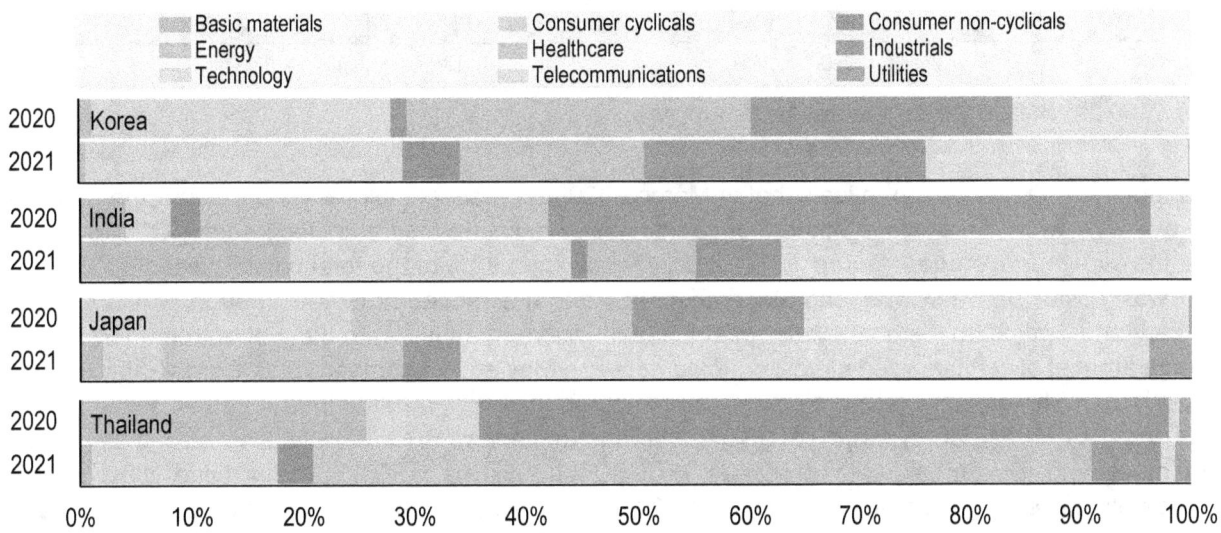

Source: OECD Capital Market Series dataset, see Annex for details.

In the period following the 2008 financial crisis, already-listed non-financial companies made extensive use of public equity markets to raise capital through secondary offerings. This trend repeated itself in 2020 and 2021, when already-listed non-financial companies raised a total of USD 626 billion and USD 645 billion via SPOs, the highest amounts in the last three decades (Figure 2.7). Asian non-financial companies raised a total of USD 250 billion in 2020 and USD 301 billion in 2021, 40% and 47% respectively of the global amounts. Notably, SPOs conducted by Chinese non-financial companies represented 60% of the capital raised by Asian companies in 2020, increasing to 62% in 2021. Companies in advanced Asia raised USD 72 billion in 2020 and USD 81 billion in 2021, representing 29% and 27% of the total Asian proceeds,

CORPORATE FINANCE IN ASIA AND THE COVID-19 CRISIS © OECD 2022

respectively. Companies from emerging and developing Asia (excluding China) raised the remaining 10% in 2020 and 2021.

Figure 2.7. Monthly secondary public offerings by non-financial companies

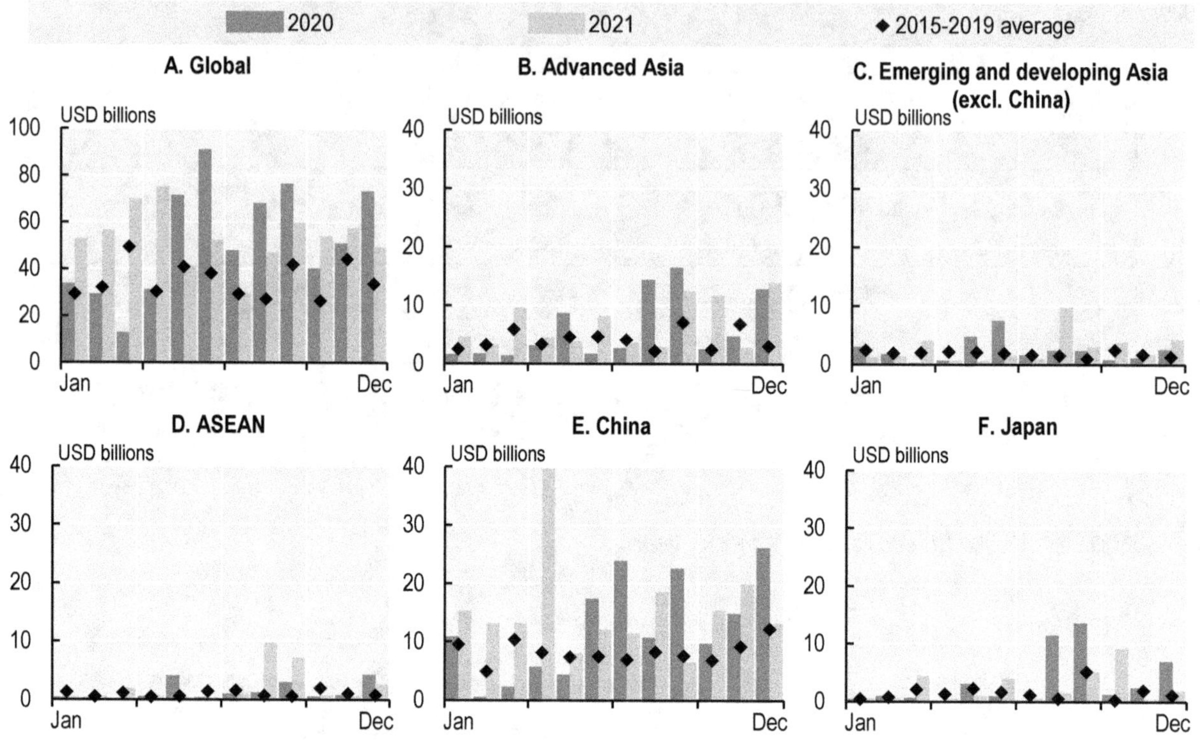

Source: OECD Capital Market Series dataset, see Annex for details.

The monthly SPO distribution reveals that in March 2020, the proceeds globally were below the past five-year average, while the average amount of capital raised between May and December 2020 was almost twice the five-year averages (Figure 2.7). Globally, more than 80% of the total capital raised via SPOs in 2020 was raised between May and December. In Asia, the proceeds raised through SPOs between February and April 2020 were below the past five-year average. In line with the global trend, the monthly average amount of capital raised almost doubled between May and December 2020. Remarkably, in India, almost USD 12 billion were raised by non-financial companies in May and June together, more than six times the past five-year average of USD 1.9 billion. In Japan, SPO activity was strong in August, September and December, with proceeds of USD 11.5 billion, USD 13.6 billion and USD 7 billion, respectively. In seven out of the 12 months of 2020, SPO activity in ASEAN economies was lower than in the 2015-19 period, although in September and December alone, the amount of capital raised was USD 3 billion and USD 4.2 billion, respectively.

As previously mentioned, SPO activity remained high in 2021. From January to April 2021 alone, the proceeds raised in Asia were greater than in the whole of 2020. During the first four months of 2021, companies from advanced Asia raised a total amount of USD 22 billion against USD 7.8 billion over the same period in 2020. Similarly, in China, at USD 81 billion the capital raised from January to April 2021 was four times larger than the same period in 2020, at USD 19 billion. Importantly, in August and September of 2021 alone, ASEAN companies raised a total amount of USD 17 billion through SPOs.

Similar to IPOs, SPOs were dominated by non-financial companies from emerging and developing Asia and mainly driven by Chinese companies. In 2020, the share of SPOs by advanced Asian companies was only around 29% of the total amount raised in the region. An annual comparison of SPOs with the previous five years reveals important differences in how companies made use of equity markets via SPOs during the COVID-19 crisis (Figure 2.8). Chinese non-financial companies raised 51% more funds compared to the previous five-year average. While Japanese IPOs contracted significantly in 2020 (as shown in Figure 2.4), SPOs by Japanese companies more than doubled. The situation was similar in Singapore, where the funds raised via SPOs were almost five times higher than the previous five-year average. In Hong Kong (China) and Indonesia, SPO activity decreased considerably, with funds raised in these jurisdictions decreasing by 50% and 70%, respectively. Malaysia, Pakistan, Philippines, Sri Lanka, Chinese Taipei, Thailand and Viet Nam, with comparatively smaller public equity markets, also experienced a contraction in the amount of funds raised in 2020. Non-financial companies from Bangladesh, Cambodia and Mongolia did not raise any funds via SPOs in 2020.

In 2021, Chinese companies raised 25% more funds via SPOs than in 2020, reaching an amount of USD 187 billion. In 2021, Japanese companies raised less capital via SPOs than in 2020 but it still exceeded the 2015-19 average and they ranked second in Asia. Notably, companies from Hong Kong (China) and Korea doubled their proceeds in 2021 compared to 2020. Similarly, Thai companies raised significant amounts of capital in 2021, totalling USD 12.5 billion, four times more than in 2020.

Figure 2.8. Secondary public offerings by Asian non-financial companies

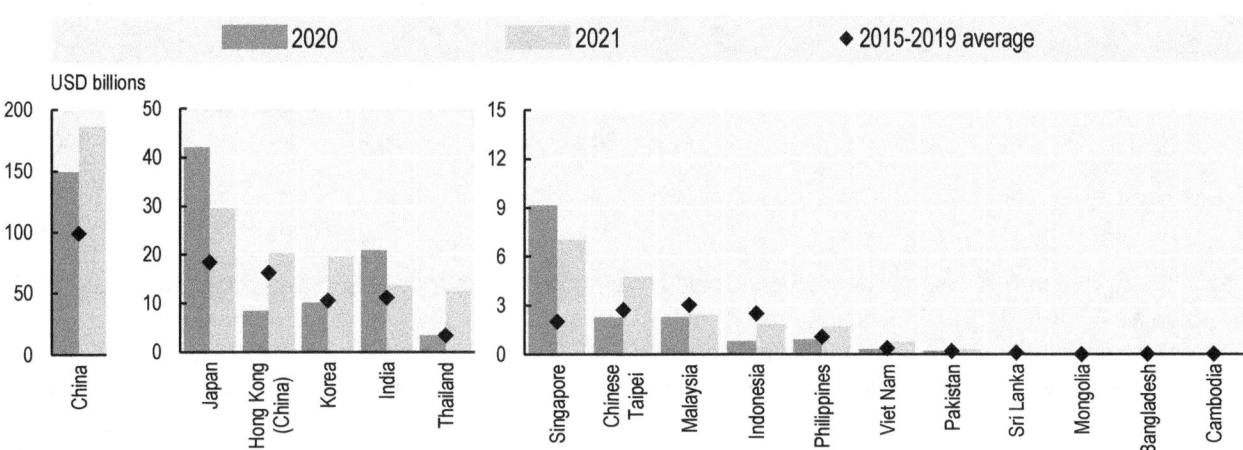

Source: OECD Capital Market Series dataset, see Annex for details.

Globally, as well as in Asia, the healthcare, industrials, technology and consumer cyclicals industries together accounted for almost 70% of all SPO proceeds in 2020 (Figure 2.9). In Asia, the top industries in terms of SPOs were industrials and consumer cyclicals, representing 24% and 16% of all SPO proceeds respectively. In advanced Asia, 35% of the proceeds were raised by industrials and 20% by telecommunications services. In emerging and developing Asia (excluding China), almost one-third of the proceeds were collected by energy companies. In China, four industries representing around 20% each were dominant, namely consumer cyclicals, industrials, healthcare and technology. Industrials and technology companies dominated secondary offerings in ASEAN economies, accounting for 42% and 20% of the proceeds raised in 2020, respectively.

In 2021, the distribution of SPOs across industries was similar to 2020 both in Asia and globally, with a slight decrease of healthcare companies and an increase of consumer cyclicals. In advanced Asia, industrial companies continued to dominate SPOs, representing 32% of total proceeds, and technology companies followed with 20%. Consumer cyclical companies accounted for 41% of the proceeds raised via SPOs in emerging and developing Asia (excluding China) in 2021, against only 8% in 2020. Healthcare companies in China raised 20% of the total proceeds in 2020 and 13% in 2021, and telecommunications companies increased from 4% in 2020 to 14% in 2021. In ASEAN economies, consumer cyclicals companies raised 45% of total SPO proceeds.

Figure 2.9. SPOs by non-financial companies by industry

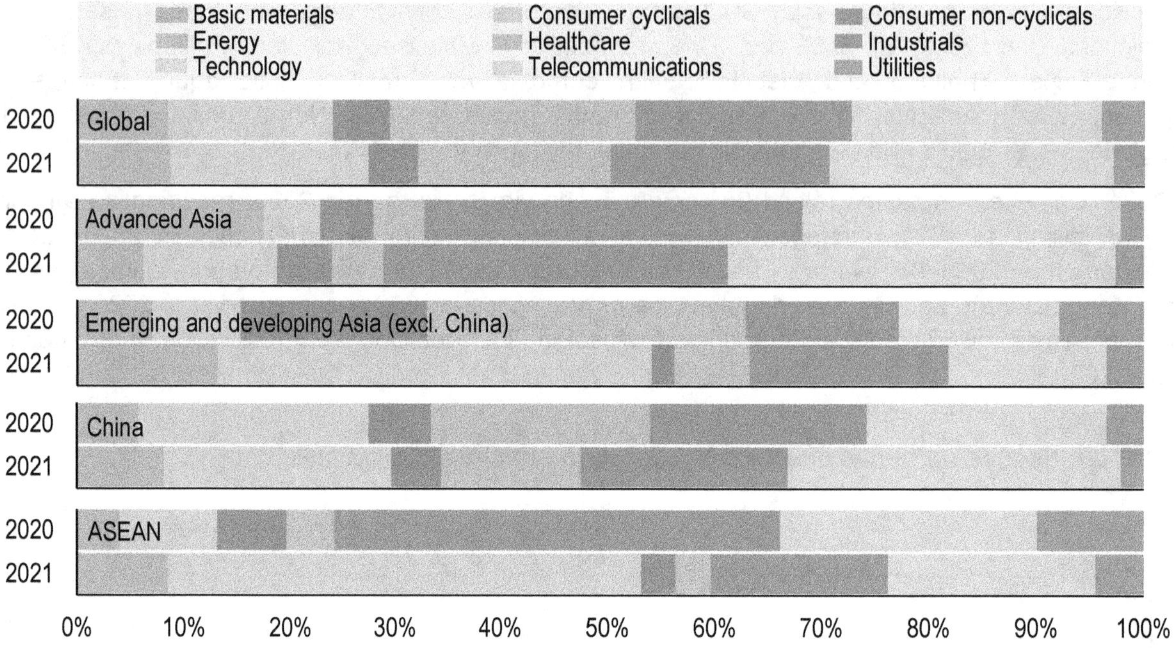

Source: OECD Capital Market Series dataset, see Annex for details.

In 2020, Japanese SPOs were mostly conducted by telecommunications (35%) and basic materials (27%) companies (Figure 2.10). The distribution changed drastically in 2021, with industrials and technology company secondary offerings dominating and raising 42% and 38% of the proceeds, respectively. While in 2020 SPOs by industrials companies from Hong Kong (China) were the most important, in 2021, 43% of the proceeds were collected by telecommunications services. Remarkably, in Korea, SPOs by industrials were important in 2020 and 2021, with 51% and 41% of the proceeds raised, respectively. In India, the energy (34%) industry was important in terms of SPOs in 2020. 2021 saw a shift in the distribution with industrials and telecommunications each accounting for almost 30%. Although utilities accounted for 39% of the proceeds raised in Thailand in 2020, in 2021, 86% of the funds were raised by consumer cyclicals.

Figure 2.10. SPOs by non-financial companies by jurisdiction and industry

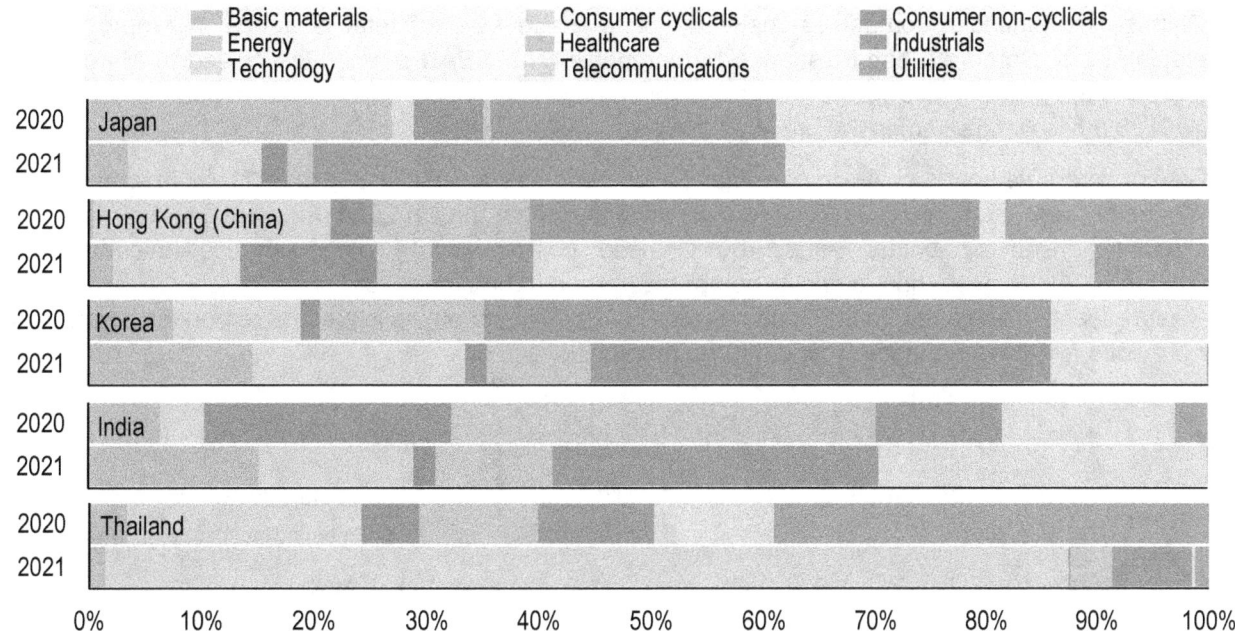

Source: OECD Capital Market Series dataset, see Annex for details.

2.1.2. Corporate bond markets

In March 2020, as the pandemic picked up pace and lockdowns began to be implemented, economic uncertainty increased sharply and companies started to face liquidity problems. In search of capital, many companies turned to the corporate bond market. In addition to meeting their immediate cash flow obligations, companies also aimed to build cushions for future economic uncertainty. Importantly, secondary corporate bond markets experienced a few weeks of disruption at the onset of the pandemic. However, central banks and governments interventions eased the pressure on the financial system improving secondary market liquidity and allowing global issuance activity to ramp up quickly in March (BIS, 2020[17]).

Following the outbreak of the COVID-19 crisis, corporate bonds represented a significant source of capital for the non-financial corporate sector. In 2020 and 2021, global bond issuances by non-financial companies reached a historical peak of USD 2.9 trillion and USD 2.5 trillion, resulting in an all-time high of USD 15.3 trillion in outstanding non-financial corporate bonds at the end of 2021. Notably, one-third of the total global amount was raised by Asian non-financial companies in 2020 and 39% in 2021. The total outstanding amount in non-financial corporate bonds issued by Asian companies reached USD 3.8 trillion in 2021, almost one-fourth of the global outstanding amount.

During the first two months of 2020, bond issuance by non-financial companies across regions remained in line with their monthly averages over the 2015-19 period (Figure 2.11). In April 2020, global corporate bond issuance peaked at USD 410 billion, two and a half times the previous five-year average. The increase was mainly driven by US non-financial companies who issued an unprecedented amount of USD 222 billion in April, almost five times the previous five-year average (OECD, 2021[2]). During the same month, Asian corporate bond issuances also peaked at USD 105 billion, of which almost 74% were issued by companies from China, while only 6% were issued by companies from other jurisdictions in emerging and developing Asia. Corporate bond issuances in advanced Asia were more stable during 2020, although still above historical averages, with issuance peaking in June at almost three times the historical averages. In July, September and October, issuance in advanced Asian jurisdictions was also high compared to five-year averages. Throughout 2020, with the exception of March and November, issuance in emerging and developing Asian jurisdictions was higher than historical averages. Notably, corporate bond issuances by Chinese non-financial companies make up on average 90% of total issuance in emerging and developing Asia. Corporate bond issuance by companies in ASEAN economies halved in March 2020 compared to the previous five-year average. Issuances by ASEAN corporations saw a peak in June 2020 with USD 6.8 billion, three times the previous five-year average.

The use of corporate bonds by Asian non-financial companies was also strong in 2021. In several months non-financial corporate bond issuances were significantly higher than in 2020 (Figure 2.11). This increase was mainly driven by bonds issued by Chinese companies. In particular, in November and December 2021, Chinese non-financial companies issued 65% and 78% in excess of the previous five-year respective averages. In 2021, companies in ASEAN economies issued more bonds compared to their previous five-year averages in all but three months.

Figure 2.11. Monthly corporate bond issuance by non-financial companies

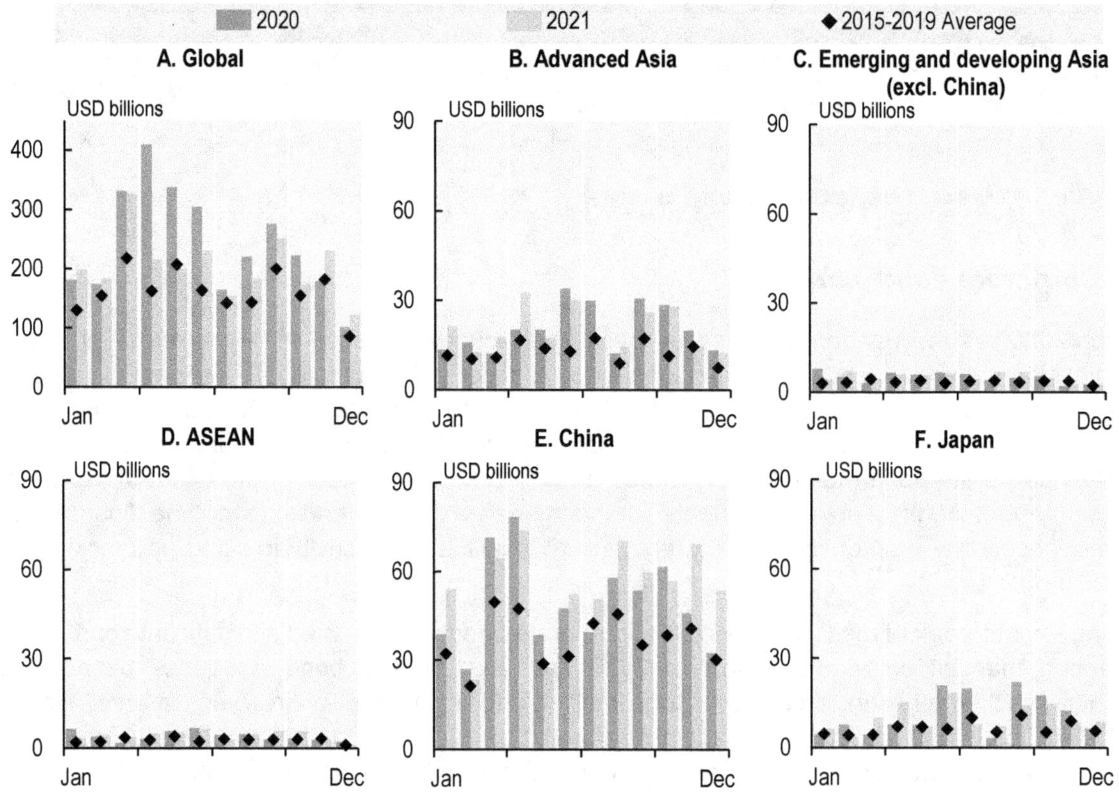

Source: OECD Capital Market Series dataset, see Annex for details.

A more detailed analysis of issuances shows important trends and differences across Asian jurisdictions. Corporate bond issuances by Chinese, Japanese and Korean non-financial companies together accounted for almost 90% of all Asian issuances in 2020, and were significantly higher than the previous five-year average (Figure 2.12). While having comparatively smaller corporate bond markets, Cambodian and Chinese Taipei companies significantly increased the issuance of corporate bonds, reaching almost six times and three times the previous five-year averages, respectively. Similarly, corporate bond issuances almost doubled in Indonesia, the Philippines and Viet Nam. In India and Singapore the increase was relatively moderate at around 30% above their previous five-year average. The use of corporate bonds by non-financial companies from Malaysia, on the other hand, remained lower than historical averages.

Non-financial companies from Mongolia and Sri Lanka did not issue corporate bonds in 2020 (although they did over 2015-19). In 2021, non-financial companies from China, Korea, Malaysia, Chinese Taipei, Thailand and Viet Nam issued higher capital via corporate bonds than they did in 2020. Importantly, for the first time in the last seven years, non-financial companies from Pakistan issued corporate bonds.

Figure 2.12. Asian non-financial corporate bond issuance by jurisdiction

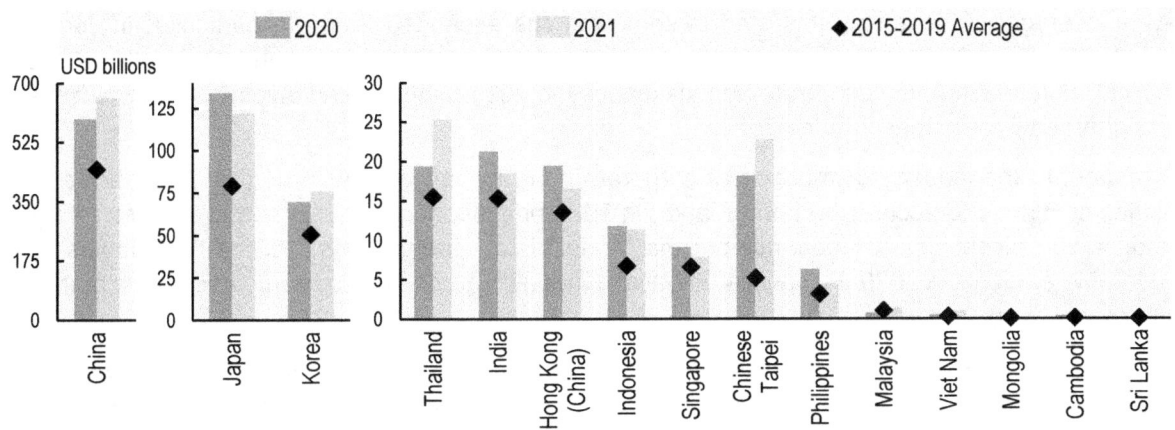

Source: OECD Capital Market Series dataset, see Annex for details.

Figure 2.13. Asian non-financial corporate bond issuance by credit quality

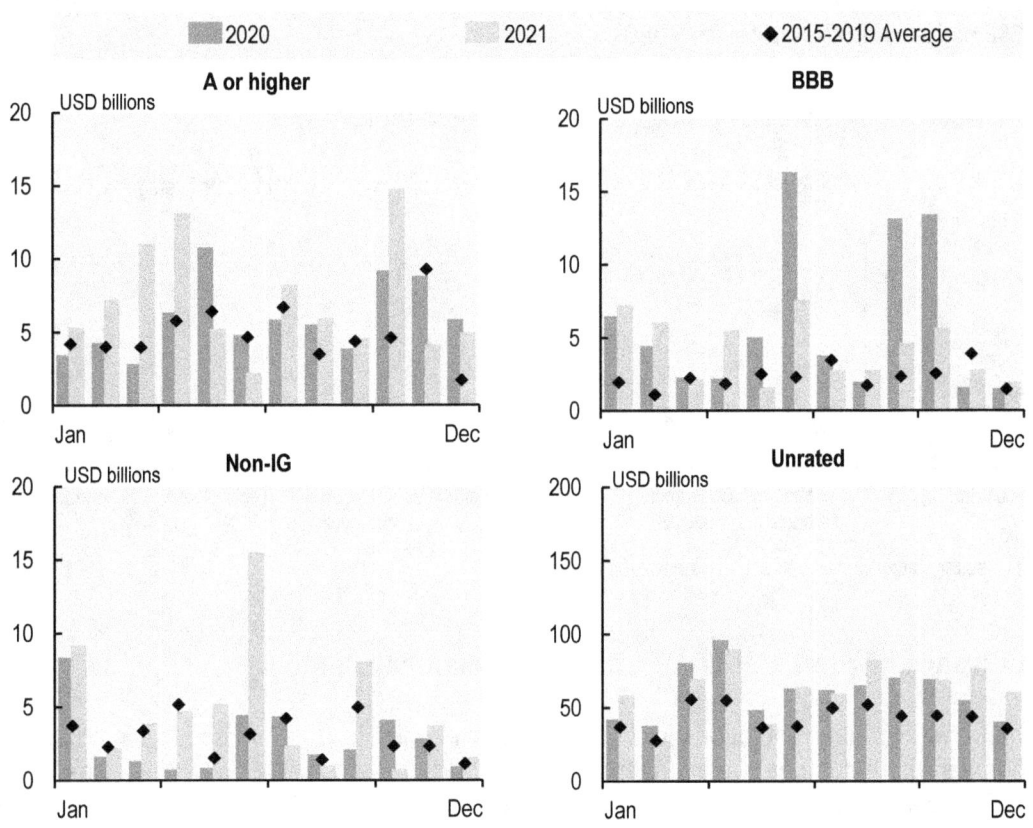

Source: OECD Capital Market Series dataset, see Annex for details.

Although, overall, corporate bond markets continued to finance companies during the crisis (Figure 2.11), a look at issuance by credit ratings underlines some important differences (Figure 2.13). As would be expected, Asian companies with investment grade ratings were impacted by the crisis to a lesser extent than non-investment grade issuers. Total issuance by non-investment grade Asian companies decreased sharply between February and May 2020, and did not increase significantly during the rest of the year. Notably, BBB rated issuances were more than five times higher than their five-year averages in June, September and October. During 2021, issuances by non-investment grade Asian companies reverted their five-year averages in seven months, and in some months exceeded them. In particular, in June 2021, issuances totalled USD 15 billion, almost five times the five-year average issuance amounts. In line with the overall increase in Asian corporate bond issuances in 2021, higher rated investment grade issuances (A or higher) saw an increase during 2021.

With respect to the industry distribution of corporate bond issuance in Asia, Figure 2.14 shows that all industries continued to access the bond market in 2020 and issuances surpassed five-year averages for all industries except for telecommunications. Industrials, energy and utilities companies issued considerable amounts in 2020. Issuances by basic materials and healthcare companies were more in line with historical averages.

Basic materials, consumer cyclicals, energy and healthcare companies issued fewer corporate bonds in 2021 than in 2020. Healthcare companies issue significantly less than in previous years. As shown in the following section, the impact of the COVID-19 crisis on aggregate sales was particularly strong in some industries, such as consumer cyclicals, energy and industrials, while the only industry with positive sales throughout 2020 was the healthcare industry (Figure 2.14). Therefore, healthcare companies did not need to issue capital via corporate bonds in 2020 and 2021. On the contrary, industrials and utilities companies continued issuing high amounts in 2021. The capital raised via corporate bonds by these industries was 42% and 6% higher than their total for 2020.

Figure 2.14. Asian non-financial corporate bond issuance by industry

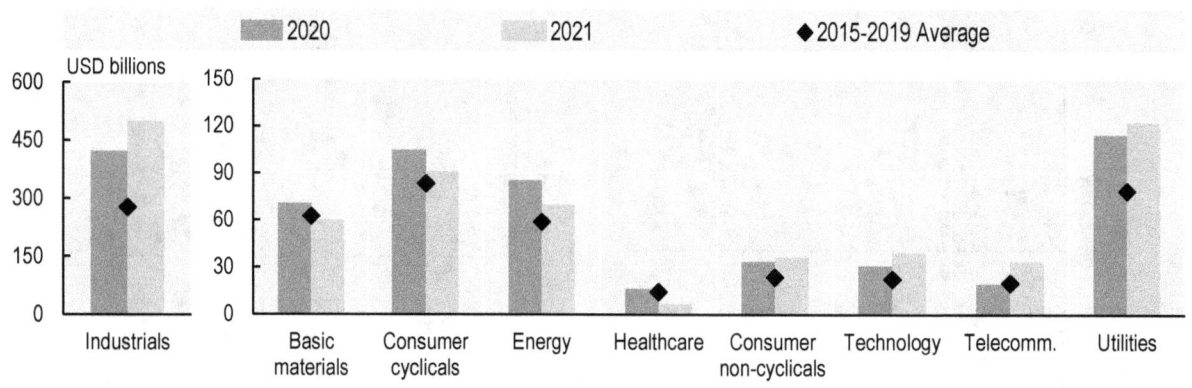

Source: OECD Capital Market Series dataset, see Annex for details.

2.2. The impact of the COVID-19 crisis on corporate sales

In 2020, the pandemic and restrictions introduced to tackle it led to a global economic crisis. As a result, most economies and industries experienced a dramatic drop in sales. Globally, the sales of the 10 000 largest non-financial listed companies dropped 4% in the first quarter of 2020 compared to the same period in 2019, 16% in the second quarter, and 5% in the third quarter (Figure 2.15). During the first quarter, listed companies in the United States were the only group of companies that did not experience a drop in sales, while in Asia and Europe sales dropped by 7% and 8%, respectively. Listed companies in Europe saw a severe contraction in sales (27%) during the second quarter.

Markets in Asia experienced various levels of contraction in sales. China was the first economy to be hit by the pandemic and experienced a decrease of 11% in the first quarter of 2020. In other Asian markets, sales dropped significantly in the second quarter. All Asian markets shown in Figure 2.15 experienced a two-digit drop except China and the rest of Asia group. Sales of listed corporations decreased by 40% in India, 20% in Korea, 18% in Japan and 21% in ASEAN.

Sales recovered globally in the third and fourth quarters of 2020, and in the fourth quarter aggregate sales increased slightly by 3%. In Asia and the United States, listed corporations recorded a 5% increase in sales, while the European corporate sector still experienced a 1% decline. It is worth mentioning that among all markets, China and the rest of Asia group saw the most vibrant recoveries, with both regions recording a 15% increase in the fourth quarter compared to 2019.

The impact of the pandemic on corporate sales lessened in 2021, with the aggregate sales of the 10 000 largest companies recovering consistently. At the global level, the first three-quarters of 2021 saw double-digit growth compared to the corresponding quarters in 2019, indicating a strong economic recovery. However, the recovery has been uneven. While the corporate sector in Asia and the United States have experienced an average increase of 15%, listed corporations in Europe have seen much smaller increases.

Asia also experienced an unbalanced recovery. Chinese corporations have seen the strongest growth, at over 30% in each quarter of 2021. The rest of Asia group experienced a similar strong recovery, with companies in Chinese Taipei recovering particularly strongly. Meanwhile, the performance of the Japanese corporate sector has been sluggish. The first quarter of 2021 saw a 3% increase in sales but they fell in the two following quarters. Listed corporations in Korea had a robust recovery, recording sales growth of 12%, 8% and 17% for the first three-quarters of 2021, respectively.

Figure 2.15. The COVID-19 crisis' impact on sales of listed corporations by economy/region

	Q1 2020	Q2 2020	Q3 2020	Q4 2020	Q1 2021	Q2 2021	Q3 2021
Global	-4%	-16%	-5%	3%	11%	11%	14%
United States	0%	-9%	1%	5%	14%	15%	18%
Europe	-8%	-27%	-12%	-1%	2%	1%	6%
Asia	-7%	-13%	-4%	5%	14%	15%	14%
China	-11%	-2%	4%	15%	32%	36%	36%
Japan	-5%	-18%	-10%	-1%	3%	-1%	-5%
India	-7%	-40%	-14%	-4%	7%	-3%	9%
Korea	-4%	-20%	-5%	2%	12%	8%	17%
ASEAN	-2%	-21%	-14%	-3%	3%	12%	1%
Rest of Asia	-5%	-1%	5%	15%	27%	25%	27%

Note: The figure reports the changes in sales between each quarter on the top row and the corresponding 2019 quarter. Sales in the figure are aggregated by economy/region using the revenues reported by companies in the interim quarterly reports. The analysis covers the largest 10 000 non-financial listed companies worldwide.
Source: OECD Capital Market Series dataset, Thomson Reuters Datastream, see Annex for details.

The impact of the COVID-19 crisis on aggregate sales was particularly severe in some industries, such as consumer cyclicals, energy and industrials. As shown in Figure 2.16, the energy industry experienced a contraction of almost 40% in sales during the second quarter of 2020, followed by a 26% and 15% decline in the third and fourth quarters, respectively. Despite the recovery in 2021, the sales of energy companies only grew in the third quarter (15%). Consumer cyclicals also witnessed significant 13% and 25% declines in sales during the first and second quarters of 2020, respectively. Meanwhile, consumer non-cyclicals corporations experienced a modest fall during the second quarter of 2020, and sales of technology and healthcare companies remained almost unchanged. Starting from the third quarter of 2020, these three industries began to see robust sales growth, which became even stronger in 2021 with double-digit growth in almost all quarters. It is also worth mentioning that basic materials companies showed the most significant sales increase in 2021, largely driven by the surge in commodity prices.

Figure 2.16. The COVID-19 crisis' impact on sales of listed companies by industry in Asia

	Q1 2020	Q2 2020	Q3 2020	Q4 2020	Q1 2021	Q2 2021	Q3 2021
Basic materials	-7%	-8%	-2%	12%	27%	32%	38%
Cons. cyclicals	-13%	-25%	-7%	4%	4%	4%	-4%
Cons. non-cyclicals	2%	-2%	1%	6%	14%	11%	8%
Energy	-13%	-39%	-26%	-15%	-1%	0%	15%
Healthcare	-2%	-1%	4%	11%	19%	18%	17%
Industrials	-8%	-10%	-4%	6%	13%	17%	15%
Technology	-1%	1%	5%	14%	27%	26%	20%
Utilities	-5%	-8%	-5%	-2%	8%	-4%	3%

Note: The figure reports the changes in sales between each quarter on the top row and the corresponding 2019 quarter. Sales in the figure are aggregated by industry using the revenues reported by companies in the interim quarterly reports. The analysis covers the largest 10 000 non-financial listed companies worldwide.
Source: OECD Capital Market Series dataset, Thomson Reuters Datastream, see Annex for details.

2.3. Government support programmes and regulatory measures in Asian economies

The COVID-19 crisis has put many companies and entire industries under severe financial pressure. As a consequence of extraordinary circumstances beyond their control, otherwise sound businesses often found it difficult to meet their obligations, for example with respect to payments and disclosure. To help them navigate the crisis, all economies adopted a range of measures spanning from regulatory adjustments to both indirect and direct financial support. Government support has been crucial and underpinned the recovery from the crisis. Appropriately, such support measures have been and continue to be large. Companies themselves have also put in place measures to cope with the situation and to respond to demands from shareholders and stakeholders.

Several of these measures were temporary in nature and introduced for the purpose of mitigating the immediate impact of the crisis. However, some of these measures may also have a long-term and lasting impact on how companies are governed, their capital and ownership structures and how they manage their relationships with shareholders and stakeholders. Certain measures may also affect the day-to-day activities of companies with respect to corporate reporting practices and the procedures for decision-making, including shareholder meetings.

This section provides an overview of regulatory and financial support measures related to corporate governance and corporate finance, focusing on large companies (and not directly targeted at SMEs). The information is summarised in a set of tables and the commentary illustrates different approaches to support measures and related initiatives. It is important to note that, as circumstances evolve, economies continue to consider adjustments of policies and regulations.

2.3.1. Government support programmes

Governments have implemented a large range of measures to support the corporate sector during the crisis. Some have provided general support whereas others have focused their efforts on the most affected industries. These measures are classified as either indirect or direct support measures.

Indirect measures

The majority of indirect measures have aimed to alleviate and ease the liquidity needs of corporations. To this end, authorities have notably provided payment deferral for tax obligations or simply lowered tax ratios. For example, a large number of jurisdictions introduced a deferral or reduction in corporate income taxes. Indonesia implemented permanent reductions of the corporate income tax (CIT) rate from 25% to 22% in 2020-21 and 20% starting in 2022. Viet Nam cut CIT for 2020 by 30% for all business with revenue below a certain threshold, and extended the payment deadline for CIT by five months. The Philippines reduced the CIT rate from 30% to 25% effective beginning July 2020 followed by a 1% annual reduction beginning January 2023 until the rate is reduced to 20% beginning January 2027. Singapore granted a CIT rebate of 25%, capped at SGD 15 000 (Singapore dollar), equivalent to USD 10 700 for 2020, and an automatic extension of interest-free instalments of two months for payment of CIT. In Chinese Taipei, higher deductions for certain salary expenses were allowed for CIT purposes.

Economies implemented a variety of other tax support measures. Some accelerated VAT refunds. For example, Indonesia accelerated VAT refunds in 19 manufacturing sectors, and Pakistan's relief measures included PKR 100 billion accelerated tax refunds to export industries. Some jurisdictions implemented measures to facilitate late tax payment. For example, Malaysia allocated RM 2.4 billion to ease financial stress on businesses through remissions of penalties related to late payment, and in Chinese Taipei, companies facing difficulties to settle tax payments could request a payment extension or payment plan. Chinese Taipei also exempted subsidies offered by the authorities to enterprises from income tax. Singapore expanded the Double Tax Deduction for Internationalization (DTDi) scheme by including new categories of expenses.

Many economies also supported companies through measures targeting social security contributions. Some cut contributions. In China, social insurance payments were cut by RMB 1 trillion (Renminbi) to incentivise companies to retain employees and RMB 4 trillion were allocated to cover payment relief for enterprises of their contributions to social security schemes. In Thailand, the rate of social security contribution was temporarily reduced to 4% of each employee's monthly salary under a certain threshold. And in India, the government paid the employee provident fund contribution both of the employee and employer of companies above a certain number of employees and salary average.

Other economies have allowed the deferment of social contribution payments. In the Philippines, the Contribution Condonation Penalty Programme allowed employers to pay overdue contributions in full or by instalment over 4 to 24 months without penalty. In Malaysia, employers were allowed to defer payments and to restructure and reschedule their contributions to the Employees Provident Fund. In Chinese Taipei, companies were allowed to defer labour insurance premium and pension payments without penalty, and in Viet Nam affected companies were allowed to defer contributions to the pension fund by up to three months without interest penalty. Cambodia also allowed the deferral of compulsory payments to the Social Security Fund in some sectors during the period of business suspension, and Mongolia's support included both an exemption on social insurance and a social insurance penalty exemption.

Some economies have also used subsidies to support companies. These subsidies have included support with utility and rent payments to facilitate business continuity. Hong Kong (China), Indonesia, Malaysia and Viet Nam, for example, reduced electricity payments. In Malaysia, tiered discounts of between 15% to 50% on electricity bills were provided to businesses for monthly consumption of up to certain level. In Hong Kong (China), a subsidy was allocated to eligible non-residential account holders to cover 75% of their monthly electricity subject to a monthly cap. Viet Nam also cut electricity tariffs to support firms affected by COVID-19, and Indonesia included vulnerable commercial sectors in its electricity bill relief subsidy.

Jurisdictions have also provided support for rent payments; they include Hong Kong (China), Indonesia, Japan, Malaysia and the Philippines. Hong Kong (China) provided rental concessions for eligible tenants of government properties and full rental waivers for businesses that had to completely cease operations due to anti-epidemic measures during the closure period. Japan's second FY2020 draft supplementary budget included subsidies to affected firms for their rent payments. In Malaysia, the government provided a special tax deduction to any company that provided a reduction of rental on business premises of at least 30%, and the Philippines implemented a minimum 30-day grace period on commercial rents of leases not permitted to work. Indonesia decreased lease charges on state-owned property for certain business and Singapore's support to businesses also included rental relief for commercial properties. In Mongolia, support to vulnerable businesses included both a rental relief and a write-off of payments of utility bills (electricity, heat, water and waste bills).

Table 2.1. Indirect measures in response to COVID-19

	Corporate income tax (deferral or lowering)	Social security contributions (deferral, waiver or lowering)	Rent and utility subsidies	Wage subsidies
Bangladesh	○	●	○	●
Cambodia	●	●	○	●
China	●	●	○	○
Hong Kong (China)	○	○	●	●
India	●	●	○	○
Indonesia	●	●	●	○
Japan	●	●	●	○
Korea	●	●	○	○
Malaysia	●	●	●	●
Mongolia	●	●	●	○
Pakistan	○	○	●	●
Philippines	●	●	●	●
Singapore	●	○	●	●
Sri Lanka	●	○	●	●
Chinese Taipei	●	●	○	○
Thailand	●	●	●	○
Viet Nam	●	●	●	○

Source: ADB (2021[18]), ADB COVID-19 Policy Database, https://COVID-19policy.adb.org/; IMF (2021[19]), IMF Policy Responses to COVID-19, https://www.imf.org/en/Topics/imf-and-COVID-19/Policy-Responses-to-COVID-19; KPMG (2020[20]), KPMG government Response – Global landscape:, https://home.kpmg/xx/en/home/insights/2020/04/government-response-global-landscape.html; IIF (2022[21]) IIF COVID-19 Global Policy Response Summary, https://www.iif.com/COVID-19; EY (2021[22]), EY Tax COVID-19 Response Tracker, https://www.ey.com/en_gl/tax/how-COVID-19-is-causing-governments-to-adopt-economic-stimulus-.

A number of economies have also supported business through wage subsidies. Malaysia introduced a Wage Subsidy Programme allowing employers to apply for staff wages subsidy of up to RM 1 200 (Malaysian ringgit) per employee for three months, under a number of conditions. Bangladesh set up a Special Fund for Salary support for export oriented manufacturing industry workers. The State Bank of Pakistan enhanced its refinance limit to finance up to 100% of wages and salaries of businesses with average three-month bill of up to PKR 500 million (Pakistani rupee). In Hong Kong (China), the Employment Support Scheme of HKD 80 billion (Hong Kong dollar) provided wage subsidies to eligible employers to retain their employees. In Singapore, the Jobs Support Scheme provided cash grants of up to the first SGD 4 600 gross monthly salary for each local employee to employers in certain industries.

Direct measures

Governments have also provided different types of direct support to companies. The most common measures have been loans and government loan guarantees. Concerning loans, Korea, for example, created a Corporate Bond-Backed Lending Facility as a lending scheme providing KRW 10 trillion (South Korean won) in loans to businesses (and banks and non-bank financial institutions). Korea also provided KRW 1.65 trillion in loans by policy banks as part of a financial aid package for the auto industry consisting of KRW 175 billion in loans and KRW 1 trillion in working capital loans with preferential interest rates for subcontractors. In Singapore, government support included a side loan capital of SGD 22 billion to help businesses facing cash flow challenges with loan obligations and insurance premium payments, as well as a SGD 4 billion bridge loan facility to Singapore Airlines (SIA). Thailand and Viet Nam also provided loans to their flag carriers. In Sri Lanka, the Saubagya COVID-19 Renaissance Facility provides a 4% working capital loan for two years (with 6-month debt moratorium) to large enterprises in affected sectors through a re-financing facility by the Central Bank.

Many jurisdictions have also provided loan guarantees. In Hong Kong (China), key measures to provide financial relief included enhancing the 80 and 90% government guarantee products by raising the maximum loan amount, providing interest subsidy, and extending the eligibility coverage to listed firms. Malaysia set up a RM 50 billion fund for working capital loan guarantees for all COVID-19 affected businesses, and India's support measures included a collateral-free lending programme with 100% guarantee. In the Philippines, the second stimulus package, "Bayanihan II", included equity to the Philippine Guarantee Corporation for its credit guarantee programmes in support of large companies, and the Central Bank assigned zero weight risk to loan exposures guaranteed by the Guarantee Corporation. In Japan, the Financial Services Agency allowed banks to assign zero risk weights to loans guaranteed with public guarantee schemes. Other examples include Indonesia where the Central Bank guaranteed working capital loans for labour intensive corporations, Cambodia where the government provided credit guarantee for business through the Business Recovery Guarantee Scheme, and Thailand where measures designed to support and transform viable businesses for the post COVID-19 world included a special loan facility for business with a credit guarantee scheme.

Some economies also introduced measures regarding loan classification and loan restructuring. In Thailand, debt restructuring measures included the extension of the loan repayment period, provision of additional working capital, interest rate reduction, and/or the extension of the loan's maturity with lower interest rates that match an expected declining post-pandemic income profile. The State Bank of Vietnam issued guidelines to commercial banks to reschedule loans, reduce/exempt interest, and provide loan forbearance. The National Bank of Cambodia also issued guidelines to financial institutions on loan restructuring for borrowers experiencing financial difficulties (but still performing) in priority sectors (tourism, garments, construction, transportation and logistics). The Central Bank of Malaysia implemented measures temporarily easing regulatory and supervisory compliance on banks to enable them to support loan deferment and restructuring, and Indonesia's Financial Services Authority relaxed loan classification and loan restructuring procedures for banks to encourage loan restructuring. China increased tolerance for higher NPLs for loans by epidemic-hit sectors and reduced NPL provision coverage requirements.

Another type of support was grants. The Monetary Authority of Singapore (MAS), AMTD Group and AMTD Foundation provided a SGD 6 million grant to support Singapore-based FinTech firms. In Indonesia, stimulus packages comprised grants for hard-hit enterprises in tourism and creative industries, and Hong Kong (China) also provided relief grants for hard-hit sectors.

Some economies also established funds or increased the amount available in existing funds in order to buy securities issued by companies. The Bank of Japan (BoJ) increased its annual pace of purchases of

Exchange Traded Funds (ETFs) and Japan-Real Estate Investment Trusts (J-REITs) up to about JPY 12 trillion (Japanese yen), equivalent to 2.2% of GDP, and JPY 180 billion (0.03% of GDP), respectively. The BoJ also dropped from the policy statement its reference to a JPY 6 trillion target for annual purchases of ETFs, while keeping the upper limit of about JPY 12 trillion, and announced that it would conduct purchases of assets such as ETFs with greater flexibly.

In Korea, the government set up a bond market stabilisation fund to purchase corporate bonds, commercial papers and financial bonds, and created a special purpose vehicle (SPV) to purchase corporate bonds and commercial papers. Korea also set up an equity market stabilisation fund (KRW 10.7 trillion) financed by financial holding companies, leading financial companies, and other relevant institutions, to invest in companies in the KOSPI 200 index. In Thailand, the Thai Bankers' Association, Government Savings Bank, insurance companies and Government Pension Fund established together a Corporate Bond Stabilisation Fund (BSF) to inject liquidity via bond rollover by providing bridge financing of up to THB 400 billion (Thai baht) to high-quality firms with bonds maturing during 2020-21, at higher-than-market 'penalty' rates. Malaysia, as part of its Short-term National Economic Recovery Plan (PENJANA), created an investment fund, amounting to MYR 1.2 billion (Malaysian ringgit), to match institutional private capital investment with selected venture capital and early stage tech fund managers.

In some cases economies decided to inject capital into affected corporations. For example, Indonesia's national economic recovery programme included capital injections into state-owned enterprises. In other cases, capital injections targeted certain strategic companies, including airlines. State-owned Korea Development Bank invested KRW 800 billion into the parent company of Korean Air Lines to help fund its takeover of Asiana Airlines. Singapore's SGD 19 billion rescue package for SIA included SGD 5.3 billion in equity. In Indonesia, Garuda issued IDR 8.5 trillion in 7-year mandatory convertible bonds to be purchased by a state-owned investment firm as part of the government's rescue plan for the airline. In Hong Kong (China), the government invested HKD 27.3 billion in Cathay Pacific through the Land Fund, which notably comprised preference shares with detachable warrants. The rescue plan for Vietnam Airlines included the issuance of VND 8 trillion (Vietnamese dong) in new shares (of which 85% will be purchased by the government's holding company, State Capital Investment Corp.).

Support to the airline industry extended beyond capital injections. The rescue package for SIA also included SGD 9.7 billion convertible note portions of SIA's fundraising underwritten by state-investor Temasek Holdings, as well as a SGD 4 billion bridge loan facility from DBS Bank. The rescue package for Vietnam Airlines also included a VND 4 trillion soft loan. The Vietnamese Government also provided loan guarantees to some aviation businesses and a discount on fees and services for domestic flights. In China, ten major air transport companies received RMB 17 billion of special bailout funds from the Export-Import Bank of China, the funding mechanism established at the beginning of 2020 to support companies stricken by COVID-19 and trade frictions with a focus on sectors related to foreign trade and manufacturing. In Cambodia, all airlines registered locally were temporarily exempted from minimum tax and were allowed to delay the payment of aviation fees, and in the Philippines, airport fees for domestic carriers were temporarily waived.

Many economies put in place targeted measures to support a large range of key industries beyond airlines. In India, for example, the Production Linked Incentive scheme targets 13 priority sectors (and is expected to cost about 0.8% of GDP over five years), and the Emergency Credit Line Guarantee scheme provides liquidity support to 26 stressed sectors by providing collateral free and 100% guaranteed loans. In Korea, a key industry stabilisation fund established for KRW 40 trillion (2.1% of GDP) and operated by Korea Development Bank was set up to support seven key industries (airlines, shipping, shipbuilding, autos, general machinery, electric power and communications). In Bangladesh, the Ministry of Finance implemented a BDT 50 billion (Bangladeshi taka) (USD 588 million) stimulus package for exporting industries channelled through Bangladesh Bank and distributed by the commercial banks at a 2% service charge. The State Bank of Vietnam asked credit institutions to channel credit to five priority sectors.

Many Asian economies have also provided a large range of support to the tourism industry, a vital industry for many of them and one of the hardest hit by the crisis. In Cambodia, for example, businesses in a number of provinces and cities were exempted from monthly tax payments and allowed to defer monthly instalment of annual tax on income liability, and funding was allocated for wage subsidies and training programmes for suspended workers in the sector. In addition, the National Bank of Cambodia issued guidelines to financial institutions on loan restructuring for borrowers experiencing financial difficulties (but still performing) from the sector (and four others). In Sri Lanka, under the government's post COVID-19 relief budget, a 4% interest five-year loan with a two-year grace period was made available to companies registered under the Sri Lanka Tourism Development Association to pay salaries of staff. In Indonesia and Malaysia, recovery measures for the tourism sector notably comprised tax reliefs.

Table 2.2. Direct measures in response to COVID-19

	Loans and loan guarantees	Subsidies	Capital injections	Business support fund	Industry targeted measures	Tourism sector support	Aviation sector support	Environment & digitalisation support
Bangladesh	●	●	○	○	○	○	○	○
Cambodia	●	●	○	○	●	●	●	○
China	●	●	●	○	●	●	●	○
Hong Kong (China)	●	●	●	○	●	●	●	●
India	●	●	●	○	●	●	○	○
Indonesia	●	●	●	○	●	●	●	●
Japan	●	●	●	●	●	●	○	●
Korea	●	○	●	●	●	●	●	●
Malaysia	●	●	●	●	●	●	○	●
Mongolia	●	●	○	○	●	○	○	○
Pakistan	●	●	○	○	●	○	○	○
Philippines	●	●	○	○	●	●	●	○
Singapore	●	●	●	○	●	●	●	●
Sri Lanka	●	●	○	○	●	●	○	○
Taipei	○	●	●	○	●	○	○	○
Thailand	●	●	○	●	●	●	●	○
Viet Nam	●	●	●	○	●	○	●	○

Source: ADB (2021[18]), ADB COVID-19 Policy Database, https://COVID-19policy.adb.org/; IMF (2021[19]), IMF Policy Responses to COVID-19, https://www.imf.org/en/Topics/imf-and-COVID-19/Policy-Responses-to-COVID-19; KPMG (2020[20]), KPMG government Response – Global landscape:, https://home.kpmg/xx/en/home/insights/2020/04/government-response-global-landscape.html; IIF (2022[21]) IIF COVID-19 Global Policy Response Summary, https://www.iif.com/COVID-19; EY (2021[22]), EY Tax COVID-19 Response Tracker, https://www.ey.com/en_gl/tax/how-COVID-19-is-causing-governments-to-adopt-economic-stimulus-.

Economies have also used their direct support to businesses to promote specific objectives, for example with respect to the environment and digitalisation. Japan's Comprehensive Economic Measures to Secure People's Lives and Livelihoods toward Relief and Hope, worth JPY 73.6 trillion (13% of 2019 GDP), includes incentives for firms to invest in digitalisation and green technologies. Korea's recovery plan, the "Korean New Deal", includes a Digital New Deal pillar and a Green New Deal pillar. The Monetary Authority of Singapore announced in April 2020 a SGD 125 million support package funded by the Financial Sector Development Fund to sustain and strengthen financial services and FinTech capabilities, and in May 2020, the MAS and AMTD Group and AMTD Foundation made a SGD 6 million grant to support Singapore-based FinTech firms. Hong Kong (China) introduced a "Distance Programme" under the Anti-epidemic Fund to help businesses fund technology solutions and purchases, and Indonesia took measures to further strengthen financial deepening and access to financial services by facilitating collaboration between the banking industry and Fintech companies.

2.3.2. Regulatory measures

Annual general meeting

Listed companies are typically required to hold an annual general meeting within three to six months after the end of their financial year. With restrictions on social gatherings, border controls and travel restrictions, 2020 annual general meetings (AGMs) were either delayed or held in different formats. The most common measure has been for public authorities to temporarily allow companies to hold shareholder meetings through remote participation, even in cases where there is a legal provision stating that the company bylaw should have authorised the remote participation.

For example, Indonesia's Financial Services Authority extended the deadline by two months for publicly listed companies to hold annual shareholders meetings. The Bangladesh Securities and Exchange Commission (BSEC) also relaxed the requirements to hold annual and extraordinary general meetings (and board meetings) and allowed companies to use any digital means for holding meetings. In Singapore, an alternative arrangement through electronic means was authorised even where personal attendance (e.g. AGM, board of directors meeting) is required by law. In Thailand, the government removed certain limitations on electronic meetings, including a rule that required that at least one-third of the quorum be present in the same location in Thailand.

Disclosure practices

Some jurisdictions also made changes concerning requirements for the release of quarterly and annual financial reports and related accounting documents. Indonesia's Financial Services Authority extended the deadline for the release of annual financial reports by two months and the Companies Commission of Malaysia extended the deadline by three months. In the Philippines the deadline was extended by 60 calendar days. China also introduced a financial reporting extension for companies severely affected by the pandemic, and Korea lifted administrative sanctions and granted a 30-day extension on the reporting deadline to companies that applied for sanctions exemptions due to pandemic-related disruptions.

Some economies also introduced new requirements to disclose material facts, guidance and estimates related to COVID-19 risks. For instance, in India, issuers were required to incorporate a quantitative and qualitative description of the main COVID-19 related risks and uncertainties to which they are exposed, and the potential measures taken to mitigate economic exposure to the pandemic. Japan established working groups addressing the COVID-19 implications in reporting and auditing to support stakeholders' engagement and ensure proper information sharing.

Limits on foreign ownership

As some companies have experienced price distortions and significant declines in their valuations, they have become vulnerable to unsolicited foreign takeovers. There has also been concerns about non-domestic ownership in sectors critical for the response to and recovery from the crisis, in particular health-related industries and associated supply chains. Several economies already had mechanisms to protect certain domestic strategic assets from foreign acquisition before the crisis. As a response to it, a number have adjusted their screening mechanisms and control rules for foreign direct investments (FDI) in order to prevent potential acquisitions of strategic assets.

Japan lowered the value of deals that triggers FDI reviewing mechanisms and modified further the associated procedural rules. India broadened the list of countries by mandating government approval for all FDI inflows from countries that share land borders with India. Conversely, for debt investments, China has instead moved towards allowing more foreign investment, lifting the restriction on foreign debt quotas that normally apply to Chinese enterprises in order to enhance liquidity.

Access to capital markets

Capital markets play a critical role in linking companies seeking capital and investors supplying it, in helping alleviate fiscal pressure on governments, in complementing bank lending, and in supporting monetary policy actions. As a result, a number of economies implemented initiatives aimed at facilitating the use of both debt and equity capital markets.

India implemented a wide range of measures to ease access to capital. The Securities and Exchange Board of India (SEBI) temporarily eased the requirements for rights issues with regard to market capitalisation, from INR 2.5 billion to INR 1 billion (Indian rupee), as well as the minimum listing period (from 3 years to 18 months) and the minimum subscription share of the total offer required (from 90% to 75%). Companies were also permitted to list securities directly in foreign jurisdictions, and private companies listing debt securities on the stock exchange were not to be regarded as listed companies. SEBI also temporarily relaxed the norms related to broker and filing fees for rights issues, public issues and share buybacks.

Other jurisdictions also implemented a wide range of measures to ease access to capital markets. The China Securities Regulatory Commission (CSRC) removed the minimum requirement for profitability and leverage, and relaxed the pricing framework required to do secondary equity offerings aiming to facilitate capital access to listed companies. The Securities Commission Malaysia and Bursa Malaysia waived annual licensing fees for capital market licensed entities and put in place regulatory relief measures for public listed companies. Indonesia's Financial Services Authority introduced a new share buyback policy allowing listed companies to repurchase their shares without a prior shareholders' meeting and introduced limits on stock price declines. The Philippines amended the Tax Code to eliminate the tax on the sale, barter or exchange of shares of stock listed and traded through initial public offering. Viet Nam temporarily reduced by 50% the rates, fees and charges in the securities industry, banks and non-bank credit institutions to support those affected by the pandemic. The Bank of Korea created a lending programme to non-banks with corporate bonds as collateral.

Some economies also implemented measures to ease bond issuance. For example, the Chinese National Development and Reform Commission (NDRC) launched a "Bond Issuance Optimisation Circular" to support the issuance of bonds to finance pandemic-related challenges, including rollover of old debt. Bond issuance procedures were also simplified, with an extended validity period of approval documents, and a COVID-19 bond label was introduced, allowing for a faster registration process for bonds where at least 10% of the proceeds were used for pandemic containment and control measures. In Cambodia, the government, as part of measures to limit tightening in financial conditions, provided financing support via increased bond issuance by corporates, including by relaxing rules on insurers for bond investments.

Payout policy

To receive public support and ensure that corporations, in particular from the financial sector, had adequate capital buffers to withstand the crisis and continue their activities, many governments and regulators took measures to limit or stop payouts during the pandemic. Further, governments may require that companies that benefit from publicly funded support programmes use that money for certain purposes, e.g. to limit layoffs or to maintain investment. In some economies, such government support has also been made contingent on restrictions with regard to payout policies. While most economies took initiatives to restrict buybacks, some took measures to facilitate them during the crisis, with a view to providing liquidity for investors who may be dependent on such payouts. This includes India, Indonesia and Korea.

Measures to restrict payouts have primarily targeted financial institutions, banks in particular. The Bank of Thailand restricted dividend payments by financial institutions in June 2020 and removed the restriction in November 2020 with the condition that the distribution of dividends could not exceed either the previous year's payout ratio nor half of the current year's net profit. The Monetary Authority of Singapore called on locally incorporated banks headquartered in Singapore to cap their total dividends per share to 60% of the FY2019 level and offer shareholders the option to receive dividends as shares instead of cash, and urged finance companies incorporated in Singapore to also cap their total dividends per share for FY2020 at 60% of FY2019s level. The National Bank of Cambodia called for banks and financial institutions to suspend dividend payments for 2020, and Pakistan suspended bank dividends for the first two quarters of 2020. In Sri Lanka, commercial banks could not declare dividends, share buybacks or increased payments to directors until end-2020. The State Bank of Vietnam instructed credit institutions to actively reduce bonuses and salaries and adjust business plans, including not paying dividend in cash. In Korea, the Financial Services Commission (FSC) recommended that banks temporarily limit dividends within 20% of their net profits to maintain their loss absorbing capacity.

Table 2.3. Selected regulatory measures in response to COVID-19

	AGM – deadline extension and/or permission to hold hybrid/virtual	Disclosure - deadline extension for presentation of financial statements	Payout - restrictions	FDI screening – tightening of mechanism	Capital markets – ease access
Bangladesh	●	●	○	○	○
Cambodia	○	○	●	○	●
China	●	●	○	○	●
Hong Kong (China)	○	○	○	○	○
India	●	●	○	●	○
Indonesia	●	●	○	○	○
Japan	●	●	○	●	○
Korea	●	●	●	○	●
Malaysia	○	●	○	○	●
Mongolia	○	○	○	○	○
Pakistan	○	○	●	○	○
Philippines	○	●	○	○	●
Singapore	●	○	●	○	○
Chinese Taipei	○	○	○	○	○
Thailand	●	●	●	○	○
Sri Lanka	○	○	●	○	○
Viet Nam	○	○	●	○	●

Source: ADB (2021[18]), ADB COVID-19 Policy Database, https://COVID-19policy.adb.org/; IMF (2021[19]), IMF Policy Responses to COVID-19, https://www.imf.org/en/Topics/imf-and-COVID-19/Policy-Responses-to-COVID-19; KPMG (2020[20]), KPMG government Response – Global landscape:, https://home.kpmg/xx/en/home/insights/2020/04/government-response-global-landscape.html; IIF (2022[21]) IIF COVID-19 Global Policy Response Summary, https://www.iif.com/COVID-19; EY (2021[22]), EY Tax COVID-19 Response Tracker, https://www.ey.com/en_gl/tax/how-COVID-19-is-causing-governments-to-adopt-economic-stimulus-.

Insolvency frameworks

The widespread business distress caused by the COVID-19 pandemic raised concerns globally about the risk of a significant increase in bankruptcies, possibly of fundamentally economically viable firms due to e.g. sharp but temporary revenue falls, supply chain issues or unfavourable conditions on financial markets. A sudden increase in corporate bankruptcies would also run the risk of causing congestion of courts with impacts on the functioning of the legal system. In order to minimise these issues, in addition to e.g. direct fiscal support many Asian jurisdictions (and others globally) implemented temporary regulatory measures related to their insolvency frameworks in response to the pandemic (Table 2.4).

Such measures included the increases in debt thresholds for initiating bankruptcy proceedings or timelines to respond to such requests; suspension to file for bankruptcy altogether; and temporary relief for directors from their duty to prevent insolvent trading. Compared to the group of (primarily G20 and OECD) countries presented in OECD (2021[2]), the group of Asian economies presented in Table 2.4 generally implemented fewer temporary measures related to insolvency. The most common measure in the broader group, suspension to file for bankruptcy/insolvency, was implemented in 23 out of 46 economies compared to only two out of 18 Asian economies. It bears mentioning that a large number of Asian jurisdictions (and indeed globally) also implemented debt moratoria (not shown in the table), temporarily postponing principal and/or interest payments which effectively amounts to a (temporary) limitation of bankruptcies, albeit not through insolvency regulation. In some economies these measures only applied to certain types of companies. For example, in Sri Lanka, a six-month debt moratorium was extended to SMEs active within certain sectors.

Table 2.4. Insolvency and bankruptcy regulatory measures in response to COVID-19

	Extension of thresholds to respond / file bankruptcy / insolvency notice	Suspension to file for bankruptcy / insolvency	Temporary relief for directors from duty to prevent insolvent trading
Bangladesh	○	○	○
Cambodia	○	○	○
China	○	○	○
Hong Kong (China)	○	○	○
India	●	●	○
Indonesia	○	●	○
Japan	○	○	○
Korea	●	○	○
Malaysia	●	○	○
Mongolia	○	○	○
Pakistan	○	○	○
Philippines	○	○	○
Singapore	●	○	●
Sri Lanka	○	○	○
Chinese Taipei	○	○	○
Thailand	○	○	○
Viet Nam	○	○	○

Source: OECD (2021[2]), *The Future of Corporate Governance in Capital Markets Following the COVID-19 Crisis*, https://doi.org/10.1787/efb2013c-en; Web search.

References

Adalet McGowan, M., D. Andrews and V. Millot (2017), "The walking dead? Zombie firms and productivity performance in OECD countries", *OECD Economics Department Working Papers, No. 1372*, OECD Publishing, Paris, https://doi.org/10.1787/180d80ad-en. [7]

ADB (2021), "ADB COVID-19 Policy Database", https://covid19policy.adb.org/. [18]

Badoer, D. (2016), "The determinants of long-term corporate debt issuances", *The Journal of Finance*, Vol. 71/1, pp. 457-492, https://doi.org/10.1111/jofi.12264. [12]

Banerjee, R. and B. Hofmann (2018), "The rise of zombie firms: causes and consequences", *BIS Quarterly Review*, September, https://www.bis.org/publ/qtrpdf/r_qt1809g.htm. [3]

Becker, B. and V. Ivashina (2014), "Cyclicality of credit supply: Firm level evidence", *Journal of Monetary Economics*, Vol. 62, pp. 76-93, https://doi.org/10.1016/j.jmoneco.2013.10.002. [13]

BIS (2020), "Corporate credit markets after the initial pandemic shock", https://www.bis.org/publ/bisbull26.htm. [17]

Çelik, S., G. Demirtaş and M. Isaksson (2015), "Corporate bonds, bondholders and corporate governance", https://www.oecd-ilibrary.org/governance/corporate-bonds-bondholders-and-corporate-governance_5js69lj4hvnw-en. [11]

De La Cruz, A., A. Medina and Y. Tang (2019), "Owners of the World's Listed Companies", *OECD Capital Market Series, Paris*, http://www.oecd.org/corporate/Owners-of-the-Worlds-Listed-Companies.htm. [14]

Denis, D. (2014), "Debt covenant renegotiations and creditor control rights", *Journal of Financial Economics*, Vol. 3/113, pp. 348-367. [6]

ECB (2021), *ECB Statistical Data Warehouse*, https://sdw.ecb.europa.eu/reports.do?node=1000002347. [10]

EY (2021), "EY Tax COVID-19 Response Tracker", https://www.ey.com/en_gl/tax/how-covid-19-is-causing-governments-to-adopt-economic-stimulus--. [22]

Fortune India (2021), "Fortune 500 India: India Inc. sweeps profits amid revenue decline", https://www.fortuneindia.com/long-reads/fortune-500-india-india-inc-sweeps-profits-amid-revenue-decline/106305. [5]

IIF (2022), "IIF COVID-19 Global Policy Response Summary", https://www.iif.com/COVID-19. [21]

IMF (2021), "IMF Policy Responses to COVID-19", https://www.imf.org/en/Topics/imf-and- [19]

covid19/Policy-Responses-to-COVID-19.

KPMG (2020), "KPMG Government Response – Global landscape", https://home.kpmg/xx/en/home/insights/2020/04/government-response-global-landscape.html. [20]

Lee, M. et al. (2013), "Economic Impact of Eurozone Sovereign Debt Crisis on Developing Asia", *ADB Economics Working Paper Series, No. 336*, https://www.econstor.eu/bitstream/10419/109446/1/ewp-336.pdf. [4]

OECD (2022), *Good Policies and Practices for Corporate Governance of Company Groups in Asia*, https://www.oecd.org/daf/ca/good-policies-practices-for-corporate-governance-company-groups-in-asia.htm. [15]

OECD (2021), *The Future of Corporate Governance in Capital Markets Following the COVID-19 Crisis*, OECD Publishing, Paris, https://doi.org/10.1787/efb2013c-en. [2]

OECD (2020), *Duties and Responsibilities of Boards in Company Groups, Corporate Governance*, Corporate Governance, OECD Publishing, Paris, https://doi.org/10.1787/859ec8fe-en. [16]

ONS (2021), *UK Economic Accounts: institutional sector - non-financial corporations*, https://www.ons.gov.uk/economy/nationalaccounts/uksectoraccounts/datasets/unitedkingdomeconomicaccountssectornonfinancialcorporations. [9]

Rauh, J. (2010), "Capital structure and debt structure", *The Review of Financial Studies*, Vol. 23/12, pp. 4242-4280, https://doi.org/10.3386/w14488. [8]

UNCTAD (2021), *World Investment Report: Investing in sustainable recovery*, https://unctad.org/webflyer/world-investment-report-2021. [1]

Annex A. Methodology for data collection and classification

In this report Asia, as a region, includes the following 18 jurisdictions: Bangladesh, Cambodia, People's Republic of China, Hong Kong (China), India, Indonesia, Japan, Korea, Lao PDR, Malaysia, Mongolia, Pakistan, Philippines, Singapore, Sri Lanka, Chinese Taipei, Thailand and Viet Nam. The report follows the IMF country classification to identify advanced economies, and emerging and developing economies. In this respect, advanced Asian economies include Hong Kong (China), Japan, Korea, Singapore and Chinese Taipei, while emerging and developing Asian economies include Bangladesh, Cambodia, People's Republic of China, India, Indonesia, Lao PDR, Malaysia, Mongolia, Pakistan, Philippines, Sri Lanka, Thailand and Viet Nam.

A. Balance sheet information for non-financial listed firms

The information presented in Section 1.1 is based on the Thomson Reuters Datastream. The unbalanced panel dataset contains financial statement information for non-financial listed companies between 2005 and 2020. The universe covers 50 376 companies registered in 133 countries.

Financial information cleaning

The raw financial dataset contains several firm-year observations when a company reports for different purposes. To construct a panel with a unique firm-year observation, the following steps are applied:

- Financial companies are excluded
- Firms listed on an over-the-counter (OTC) market are excluded
- Security types classified as "units" and "trust" are excluded
- Firms identified as delisted are excluded
- For firms with multiple observations but different countries of domicile, their true country of domicile is manually checked to remove the duplicates
- Financial statements covering a 12-month period are used
- Companies with at least one observation showing negative assets or negative fixed assets are excluded
- Financial information is adjusted by annual US Consumer Price Index changes and information is reported in 2020 USD

The information presented in Section 2.2 is also based on the Thomson Reuters Datastream. The information on reported sales is collected for a representative regional sample of listed companies. Sales data reported in interim quarterly financial statements are collected for all quarters in 2019 and the ones available in 2020. Financial companies are excluded from the sample.

Industry classification

The Thomson Reuters Datastream uses Thomson Reuters Business Classification (TRBC). The economic sectors used in the analysis are listed in Table A A.1.

Table A A.1. Economic sectors based on the Thomson Reuters Business Classification

Thomson Reuters Economic Sector	
Basic Materials	Industrials
Cyclical Consumer Goods / Services	Non-Cyclical Consumer Goods / Services
Energy	Technology
Financials	Telecommunications Services
Healthcare	Utilities

B. Listing information

The information presented in Figure 1.23 is based on the OECD-ORBIS Corporate Finance database. The listing status is collected from the ORBIS *Legal Information* tables between 2008 and 2019, and is further complemented with information retrieved from Worldscope.

C. Public equity data

The information on initial public offerings (IPOs) and secondary public offerings (SPOs or follow-on offerings) presented is based on transaction and/or firm-level data gathered from several financial databases, such as Thomson Reuters Eikon, Thomson Reuters Datastream, FactSet and Bloomberg. Considerable resources have been committed to ensuring the consistency and quality of the dataset. Different data sources are checked against each other and, whenever necessary, the information is also controlled against original sources, including regulators, stock exchanges and company websites and financial statements.

Data used in Figure 1.25 classifies companies as listed on a foreign jurisdiction whenever the jurisdiction of the company's headquarter is different from the stock exchange jurisdiction where the company's shares are listed. Additionally, China in this exercise refers to mainland China and Hong Kong (China) together.

Country coverage and classification

The dataset includes information about all initial public offerings (IPOs) and secondary public offerings (SPOs or follow-on offerings) by financial and non-financial companies. All public equity listings following an IPO, including the first time listings on an exchange other than the primary exchange, are classified as a SPO. If a company is listed on more than one exchange within 180 days, those transactions are consolidated under one IPO. The country breakdown is based on the issuer's country of domicile. In the dataset, the country of issue classification is also made based on the stock exchange location of the issuer.

It is possible that a company becomes listed in more than one country when going public. The financial databases record a dual listing as multiple transactions for each country where the company is listed. However, there is also a significant number of cases where dual listings are reported as one transaction only based on the primary market of the listing. For this reason, the country breakdown based on the stock exchange is based on the primary market of the issuer.

Currency conversion, inflation adjustment and growth company threshold

The IPO and SPO data are collected on a deal basis via commercial databases in current USD values. The information presented is aggregated at the annual frequency and in some tables, presented at the year-industry level. Issuance amounts initially collected in USD were adjusted by 2021 US Consumer Price Index (CPI).

In Section 1.2, the threshold for identifying growth company IPOs – USD 100 million – is fixed in 2010 USD adjusted by US CPI. Information provided in Chapter 2 is collected and presented in current USD.

Industry classification

Initial public offering and secondary offering statistics are presented in this report using the Thomson Reuters Business Classification (TRBC). The economic sectors used in this analysis are listed in Table A A.1.

Exclusion criteria

With the aim of excluding IPOs and SPOs by trusts, funds and special purpose acquisition companies the following industry categories are excluded:

- Financial companies that conduct trust, fiduciary and custody activities
- Asset management companies such as health and welfare funds, pension funds and their third-party administration, as well as other financial vehicles
- Open-end investment funds
- Other financial vehicles
- Grant-making foundations
- Asset management companies that deal with trusts, estates and agency accounts
- Special Purpose Acquisition Companies (SPACs)
- Closed-end investment funds
- Listings on an over-the-counter (OTC) market
- Security types classified as "units" and "trust"
- Real Estate Investment Trusts (REITs)
- Transactions with missing or zero proceeds

D. Ownership data

The main source of information is the FactSet Ownership database. This dataset covers companies with a market capitalisation of more than USD 50 million and accounts for all positions equal to or larger than 0.1% of the issued shares. Data are collected as of end of 2020 in current USD, thus no currency nor inflation adjustment is needed. The data are complemented and verified using Thomson Reuters Eikon and Bloomberg. Market information for each company is collected from Thomson Reuters Eikon. The dataset includes the records of owners for 25 766 companies listed on 92 markets covering 98% of the world market capitalisation. For each of the economies/regions presented, the information corresponds to all listed companies in those economies/regions with available information.

The information for all the owners reported as of the end of 2020 is collected for each company. Some companies have up to 5 000 records in their list of owners. Each record contains the name of the institution, the percentage of outstanding shares owned, the investor type classification, the origin country of the investor, the ultimate parent name, among other things.

The table presents the five categories of owners defined and used in this report. Different types of investors are grouped into these five categories of owners. In many cases, when the ultimate owner is identified as a Government, a Province or a City and the direct owner was not identified as such, ownership records are reclassified as public sector. For example, public pension funds that are regulated under public sector law are classified as government, and sovereign wealth funds (SWFs) are also included in that same category.

Table A A.2. Categories of owners

Investor category	Investor type	
Private corporations and holding companies	Business Association	Operating Division
	Employee Stock Ownership Plan	Private Company
	Holding Company	Public Company
	Joint Venture	Subsidiary
	Non-profit organisation	
Public sector	Government	Regional Governments
	Sovereign Wealth Manager	Public Pension Funds
Strategic individuals and family members	Individual (Strategic Owners)	Family Office
Institutional investors	Bank Investment Division	Mutual Fund Manager
	Broker	Other
	College/University	Pension Fund
	Foundation/Endowment Manager	Pension Fund Manager
	Fund of Funds Manager	Private Banking/Wealth Management
	Fund of Hedge Funds Manager	Private Equity Fund/Alternative Inv.
	Hedge Fund	Real Estate Manager
	Hedge Fund Manager	Research Firm
	Insurance Company	Stock Borrowing/Lending
	Investment Adviser	Trust/Trustee
	Market Maker	Umbrella Fund
	Mutual Fund-Closed End	Venture Capital/Private Equity
Other free-float including retail investors	Shares in the hands of investors that are not required to disclose their holdings. It includes the direct holdings of retail investors who are not required to disclose their ownership and institutional investors that did not exceed the required thresholds for public disclosure of their holdings.	

E. Corporate bond data

Data presented on corporate bond issuances are based on OECD calculations using data obtained from Thomson Reuters Eikon that provides international deal-level data on new issues of corporate bonds that are underwritten by an investment bank. The database provides a detailed set of information for each corporate bond issue, including the identity, nationality and sector of the issuer; the type, interest rate structure, maturity date and rating category of the bond, the amount of and use of proceeds obtained from the issue.

Convertible bonds, deals that were registered but not consummated, preferred shares, sukuk bonds, bonds with an original maturity less than or equal to one year or an issue size less than USD 1 million are excluded from the dataset. The analyses in the report are limited to bond issues by non-financial companies. The industry classification is carried out based on Thomson Reuters Business Classification (TRBC). The country breakdown is carried out based on the issuer's country of domicile. Yearly issuance amounts initially collected in USD were adjusted by 2021 US Consumer Price Index (CPI). Information provided in Chapter 2 is collected and presented in current USD.

Given that a significant portion of bonds are issued internationally, it is not possible to assign such issues to a certain country of issue. For this reason, the country breakdown is carried out based on the country of domicile of the issuer. The advanced/emerging market classification is based on IMF country classification.

Rating data

Thomson Reuters Eikon provides rating information from three leading rating agencies: S&P, Fitch and Moody's. For each bond that has rating information in the dataset, a value of 1 to the lowest credit quality rating (C) and 21 to the highest credit quality rating (AAA for S&P and Fitch and Aaa for Moody's) is assigned. There are 11 non-investment grade categories: five from C (C to CCC+); and six from B (B- to BB+). There are ten investment grade categories: three from B (BBB- to BBB+); and seven from A (A- to AAA).

If ratings from multiple rating agencies are available for a given issue, their average is used. Some issues in the dataset, on the other hand, do not have rating information available. For such issues, the average rating of all bonds issued by the same issuer in the same year (t) is assigned. If the issuer has no rated bonds in year t, year t-1 and year t-2 are also considered, respectively. This procedure increases the number of rated bonds in the dataset and hence improves the representativeness of rating-based analyses. When differentiating between investment and non-investment grade bonds, the final rating is rounded to the closest integer and issues with a rounded rating less than or equal to 11 are classified as non-investment grade.

Early redemption data

When calculating the outstanding amount of corporate bonds in a given year, issues that are no longer outstanding due to being redeemed earlier than their maturity should also be deducted. The early redemption data are obtained from Thomson Reuters Eikon and cover bonds that have been redeemed early due to being repaid via final default distribution, called, liquidated, put or repurchased. The early redemption data are merged with the primary corporate bond market data via international securities identification numbers (i.e. ISINs).

Notes

[1] Zombie companies' definition here follows Adalet McGowan, Andrews and Millot (2017). Zombie companies are defined as firms older than 10 years that during three consecutive years are not able to cover their interest payments with their operating income. The age restriction is imposed to differentiate between real zombie firms and young innovative firms.

[2] The analysis only considers primary listing on a market different from the one where the company is domiciled as a non-domestic listing; secondary listings on a non-domestic market are not counted as non-domestic.

[3] The definition of control is based on equity shareholdings and the minimum cut-off to be considered a controlled company is if any single public sector owner holds at least 25% of the equity. The selection of 25% of the equity as a cut-off is based on the fact that most jurisdictions require at least 75% of the votes cast by shareholders to pass a special resolution. Thus a shareholder with more than 25% of the votes can block special resolutions, and is considered as a majority shareholder. This definition may differ from the one provided by the OECD SOE Guidelines, which state that "any corporate entity recognised by national law as an enterprise, and in which the state exercises ownership, should be considered as an SOE". Importantly, the OECD SOE Guidelines state: "The Guidelines apply to enterprises that are under the control of the state, either by the state being the ultimate beneficiary owner of the majority of voting shares or otherwise exercising an equivalent degree of control."

[4] The state holdings correspond to the average within the companies identified as being under state control.